Burdett Hart

Biblical Epochs

Burdett Hart

Biblical Epochs

ISBN/EAN: 9783742810151

Manufactured in Europe, USA, Canada, Australia, Japa

Cover: Foto ©Lupo / pixelio.de

Manufactured and distributed by brebook publishing software (www.brebook.com)

Burdett Hart

Biblical Epochs

BIBLICAL EPOCHS

BY

Rev. BURDETT HART, D. D.

Author of
"Aspects of Christ: Studies of the Model Life,"
"Aspects of Heaven," "Always Upward."

Ἐν πάσαις ταῖς γραφαῖς τὰ περὶ αὑτοῦ.
Λουκᾶς 24:27

PHILADELPHIA
PRESBYTERIAN BOARD OF PUBLICATION
AND SABBATH-SCHOOL WORK
1896

COPYRIGHT, 1896, BY
THE TRUSTEES OF THE
PRESBYTERIAN BOARD OF PUBLICATION
AND SABBATH-SCHOOL WORK.

All rights reserved.

In Memory

OF A BELOVED AND SAINTED

Mother

THROUGH WHOSE REVERENT AND ILLUMINANT

Teaching

I WAS MADE ACQUAINTED FROM

Earliest Childhood

WITH THE

Holy Scriptures.

PREFATORY.

The evolution of the Holy Scriptures was the slow, progressive work of ages. Revelation was not perfected by one single publication of what God would have men believe and know, but it was made by gradual steps of progress, by unfolding of truth as men were prepared to receive it. Its basal design was to develop the divine plan of salvation for mankind. This great purpose runs through it all like a band of gold through the entire woof of a costly fabric. Its occult announcement was made at the genesis of the Biblical narration; it was reiterated in type and prophecy, in signs and wonders, in sacrifice and law and poetry, until, in the fullness of time, all came to completion in the person and work and atoning death of our Lord and Saviour Jesus Christ.

The Old Testament was a preparation for the New Testament. The Hebrew history was an introduction to the gospel of the Son of God. The call of the patriarchs, the separation of the children of Israel, the theocratic government of that race through ages of history, were designed to conserve the revelation that God would make of his one great purpose to bring in the Kingdom for which the world stands. The Bible is the history of Redemption—peculiar, composite, running into significant digressions, but ever keeping a single end in view. These Scriptures are the inspired records of God's conduct of his people in their long discipline for the coming of the Christ. They are unique among the world's historic and literary works. "Men spake from God, being moved by the Holy Spirit." We are to recognize in them blended human agency and divine direction. They are the Holy Scriptures.

They are by human hands, and hence are the subject of reverent investigation. That they are in human hands implies that their transmission is under the liabilities of all human work. That they are from God implies that he would have a care for these most important of his works for mankind; and accordingly we find that the Scriptures have come to us exceptionally guarded in their content and correct in their statements.

The recent discoveries from the treasures of old libraries, from the literature of forgotten and buried collections, from the deciphered inscriptions of ancient monuments, from the guarded manuscripts of cloisters, are shedding new light on the ancient records, and are giving strange confirmation to that which has been faithfully cherished by the Church.

We are finding that the old Bible is ours; that its truthfulness is confirmed and authenticated by the results of discovery and scholarship. More and more it is proved to be our own BIBLE—the one Sacred Book of the world. Its words, sounding down all the centuries, freighted with the joys and griefs and exultant hopes and victories of saints through the past millenniums, vocal ever with the songs of angels, and full of the expression of the Son of God, are proved to be the very Word of God. The Bible is the stronghold of Christianity. All antagonisms smite at it, would gladly destroy it. It stands impregnable, the same old Bible, with the memory of the dead in it, with the warm love of childhood in it; with the woe of our trials reverberating in its melancholy experience, and the joys of our better days ringing in its psalms and prophecies, like chimes of musical bells above the lower life. Its voices are like choice music which one cannot forget; its promises are like faces that ever beam upon us in their remembered expression; it is like a life within our life, warming and refreshing and invigorating us.

Great periods hold their separate and valuable

contributions to the one object for which all Scripture was given by inspiration of God. The prominent epochs are great developments of the progressive, and often mysterious, methods by which the divine purpose was effected. They present scenes full of tragic interest, in which divine wisdom, united with human agency, moves on to the final issue.

Human history, as set forth in the Holy Scriptures, may be distinguished into Nine Great Epochs—the Paradisean, the Antediluvian, the Patriarchal, the Mosaic, the Prophetic, the Messianic, the Apostolic, that of the Holy Spirit, the Millennial. Each one presents its lessons of instruction and profit; for "every scripture inspired of God is also profitable for teaching, for reproof, for correction, for instruction which is in righteousness: that the man of God may be complete, furnished completely unto every good work." The records, carefully preserved, guarded by divine providence, furnishing lessons of wisdom to peoples who have received and cherished them all along the progress of the race, also "were written for our admonition, upon whom the ends of the ages are come." They bring to us, in ever-augmented volume, acquaintance with God's moral government, and impressive enlightenment as to our personal duty.

The range that is opened to us by these great epochs is vast and comprehensive, reaching from the golden era of the world's morning, a morning bright and beautiful and full of hope, through long periods of sin and turbulence and conflict, down to the world's gorgeous evening, when the light and songs and bliss of the early Paradisean day, shall be restored in wider radiance and sweeter harmonies and deeper happiness, during the wearily-awaited and long-protracted Millennium. We shall see the powers of evil at their baleful work, "spiritual hosts of wickedness" in opposition to God; we shall behold august and holy personages rising up from the dark ranks of humanity, to warn, to instruct, to bless the race; we shall see ONE, with the marks of high divinity upon him, moving forth under obloquy and hate to the rescue of the lost world; we shall witness the ongoing of a blessed agency winning and subduing mankind to God.

CONTENTS.

EPOCH	PAGE
I.—The Paradisean	11
II.—The Antediluvian	29
III.—The Patriarchal	51
IV.—The Mosaic	71
V.—The Prophetic	91
VI.—The Messianic	113
VII.—The Apostolic	147
VIII.—That of the Holy Spirit	183
IX.—The Millennial	201

EPOCH I.

THE PARADISEAN.

BIBLICAL EPOCHS.

THE PARADISEAN.

WHOSE mind has not reverted to the golden days when our first parents lived in paradise? Who that has felt the effects of sin and has seen its gloomy reign on earth has not wished that Adam had remained unfallen, in his original beauty and glory? That was indeed a state to be desired, of which now we can form only an indistinct conception.

Paradise is described in the Scriptures as a garden. The account is: "The Lord God planted a garden eastward, in Eden; and there he put the man whom he had formed." It was "the garden of the Lord," "the garden of God." Eden was a large region, whose locality, although it has been the subject of great research and speculation, is yet unknown. We may suppose it to have been, wherever situated, the finest portion of this beautiful world which God had made for the residence of man. It was a land of mountains and smiling valleys and running streams, rich in vegetation, abounding in lofty trees and fragrant flowers of varied hues. Its sky was azure and clear; its atmosphere salubrious and lucid. Over its plains and through its forests roamed in delightful harmony beasts of every species, flew birds of varied notes and brilliant plumage, dwelt all living animals, which were then content in the new life which the Creator had so recently given to them.

In the midst of this fair Eden, this land of pleasure, as the word imports, God had planted a garden. More beautiful than the picturesque country which surrounded it, designed as the agreeable dwelling place, the home, of those immortal beings, who, made in the image of their Creator, were to have dominion over the earth and all that dwelt upon it. It was the center of production and pleasure, the choice spot where the Creator had lavished his gifts, the paradise of the new world, the bright gem in the coronet of nature. There was seen a luxuriance which has never been equaled.

In this garden of God massive trees, cedars of Lebanon, "with fair branches, and with a shadowing shroud, and of an high stature," lifted to heaven their dense foliage and were swayed by the gentle gales that swept through their musical crowns. The earth teemed with richest plants of every order, whose unbroken series of fruits and flowers loaded the air with their delicate odors. Fountains of perennial waters gushed forth in every grove, imparting coolness to the air and clothing the ground with verdure. Birds of flashing plumage swept through those paradisean woods on tireless wings, waking in every bower the sweetest harmonies. Lakes, on whose bosom floated flowering lilies and over which sailed aquatic fowl, nestled in shady retreats, mirroring in their glassy waves the trees that stood like sentinels around them. In the midst of the garden rose the towering "tree of life" and by its side the "tree of the knowledge of good and evil." In this garden of delight God placed the man whom he had formed. He assigned to him his duties. For labor he was to till the ground, to perpetuate the useful productions of the earth, to supply himself with vegetable food, and to maintain the garden in its pristine beauty. God did not design man for idleness. Even in his unfallen, upright state, in the prodigality and spontaneousness of paradise, he was to develop his own constitution and the resources of nature by personal labor. Had he remained in sinless strength and purity his work would have been his pleasure, and its products would have been vigor for himself and ornaments of utility for the world.

He was also to find development in meditation and worship. In that productive garden it was easy for man to secure the supplying of his wants. His mental and moral nature would demand cultivation. He would have time for study and for communion with God.

In paradise, man was placed under law. One tree, the tree of the knowledge of good and evil, was not to be used. "The Lord God commanded the man, saying, Of every tree of the garden thou mayest freely eat: but of the tree of the knowledge of good and evil, thou shalt not eat of it: for in the day that thou eatest thereof thou shalt surely die." So, then, were the parents of our race in their Eden home, pursuing their labor, engaging in study and worship, and maintaining obedience to the law of their Maker.

We fairly may infer that these progenitors of the human family came from the hands of their Creator perfect in body and soul. They were adult, fitted in mind and body for the life they were to lead, for the duties which at once devolved upon them. Though they were children in experience, they were not immature in power. They stood in the glory of their paradisean home, vigorous and mature, the highly gifted lords of creation. They honored the handiwork of their wise Maker. As God saw that all other things which he created were very good, so he saw that man was a perfect creation, for in the image of himself did God create man: "In the image of God created he him; male and female created he them." They were the children of the heavenly Father. They did justice to his design and product. In blooming health and strength and beauty they probably far surpassed all who have succeeded them.

> "The loveliest pair
> That ever since in love's embraces met—
> Adam the goodliest man of men since born
> His sons; the fairest of her daughters Eve."

Since that, sin has wrought a deterioration in the lineaments and proportions of the human form; passion has put its stamp thereon; weakness and sickness have disarranged the harmony and beauty with which God endowed it. Man has lost the port and power of his primal manhood.

Then the soul was in its most excellent state. All its powers were in peace and harmony. There was no discord from depravity, no darkness from prejudice, no wrong sway from false habits and perverted appetites. God made men upright; their many inventions are of their own seeking. By their very constitution they were fitted for the life to which they were introduced. They were holy. They loved God. They saw in him the chief excellence, and their affection went forth spontaneously and earnestly toward him. From all the objects around them, from the wonders of the vast creation, from the loveliness of the new-formed earth, from nature in all its marvels and works, their devotion went up to nature's God. From every pleasure that thrilled their senses, from every duty that sprang from their quick delight, from every joy in their free and blessed confidence, in their unrestricted intercourse, they turned with holy trust to God and in him they found sweetest rest and peace. They had no thought, no purpose, that was opposed to God. The idea of sin was foreign to their nature, and had they not been tempted from without they probably never would have fallen.

We can reproduce in imagination somewhat of the life in paradise of the first children of God on earth. With powers all fitted for immediate activity, filled with uninterrupted happiness from all that they observed and from their personal experiences, they dwelt in the center and at the head of the new creation. Life and beauty were all around them; the life and beauty of the earth's glad morning, before the gloom of sin had enshrouded it and before the wickedness of man had polluted it with deeds of violence and crime; indeed, just as God himself with infinite skill and wisdom had formed it. There they lived alone, yet not alone; they lived amidst the works of nature which are the works of God. Every song they heard found an echo and refrain within them. Every leaf and flower was penciled with divine words, the writings of God's hand. Every star shone in its beams with the smile of God. The scenes of loveliness in the world, in all the visible universe, were photographs by God's own hand. All things on earth were subordinated to their will. God gave man dominion over the fish of the sea, and over the fowl of the air, and over every living thing that moveth upon the earth. He authorized him to subdue the earth, to bring its every treasure and product into subjection to his desires and purposes. God also caused the beasts and the fowls to pass before Adam, in long succession and order, that he might give them names, and whatsoever the man called every living creature that was the name thereof. In this vocabulary he first perhaps practically employed the language which the Creator had given him. From that he extended his observations, gained a knowledge of the properties and uses of other objects, and classified the diverse kingdoms of nature.

God was the teacher of our first parents. They had the mental and moral capacities which fitted them for intelligent and spiritual life. They had minds and bodies constituted for right action, but not matured by experience. In capacity, they were mature; in experience, immature. They were not under the necessity of growing up in stature and in mental strength; all that they needed was the right exercise of the powers which they had. This God taught them. The habits and attainments which are necessary for right living are ordinarily the product of the long and co-operative experience of men; but at first we have reason to believe that many things were communicated directly by the Creator. He assumed the education of his children, that they might enter on life in accord with his design and might properly educate their children. So the first parents were divinely instructed, and their temporal and spiritual life began as God desired.

It may be reasonable to assume that the Second Person of the glorious Trinity, the Son of God, who afterward appeared to the patriarchs, who in the fullness of time came forth as the Saviour of the race, who throughout all our human history has been brought into most intimate relations with men, was, in human form, but in divine grace, by intimate and blessed intercourse, the voluntary instructor of these earliest scholars of mankind.

Perhaps, too, holy angels communed with them; came with the Son of God on their shining pinions, walked with Adam and Eve through the fascinating grounds of paradise, telling them of God, of more brilliant mansions in the holy heaven, their home, of the occupations of those earlier children of God, and loving them as younger, the earth-born, children of the common Father.

To them everything was new. Life was new; the world was new; their acquaintance with God and with his works was new and full of mystery. They looked abroad through the long-drawn vistas of Eden and beheld forests and towering mountains and running rivers stretching away through great territories all unknown to them. They turned their gaze into the blue heavens, and their wonder was stirred by the arching sky and the stellar orbs. They must have prized the presence of superior spirits with whom they could converse and whom they could love. Happy pair! happy in themselves, happy in their home, happy in their Creator. How long they continued in their blissful state, enjoying the blessings of paradise and communing with God as their Father, we are not informed. Months and years perhaps may have passed by, during which they grew in knowledge and ability and in the full understanding of their condition and relations. During this time, short or long, they obediently observed the requirements of their Creator. Daily they ate of the tree of life which stood in the midst of the garden, whose fruit preserved their health, renewed their strength, and would have sustained them in perpetual vigor as long as they should partake of it.

At length there came a change—dark, sudden, terrible. The conspirator from hell entered paradise, and tempted Eve, in a way unknown to us, by some evil lure, to taste of the fruit of the tree of the knowledge of good and evil, of which God had said, "Thou shalt not eat of it: for in the day that thou eatest thereof thou shalt surely die." To this tree the obedient pair had never dared, never wished, to stretch forth a hand; they had not even thought of doing what their Creator had forbidden them to do. But the insidious wiles, the artful pleas, of the tempter, the adversary of God and man, were too much for the new, frail virtue of the holy, inexperienced parents of our race. The law of God was not so completely and firmly enthroned in them that temptation could not move them from their loyalty. Eve at first answered the tempter well; but by gradual advances he drew her toward the fatal act. "When the woman saw that the tree was good for food, and that it was a delight to the eyes, and that the tree was to be desired to make one wise, she took of the fruit thereof, and did eat; and she gave also unto her husband with her, and he did eat." The sinful deed was done.

From that moment the history of man was changed. Sin was in the world, and death and all our woes were secured. The curse of God was pronounced upon man. Pain and sorrow would afflict him. Thorns and thistles would spring up on the ground, increasing the burden of labor. God, who had been man's friend, who had condescended to an intimate intercourse with him, would withdraw and leave him to bitter regrets and hard endurance and the woe of sin. Death would begin its reign, a wide and terrific dominion! Yet, mingled with the sternness of justice were promises of mercy; on the clouds of despair was painted the bow of hope; and God, who pronounced the penalty, proclaimed deliverance. In the very midst of the sorrows of the Fall came the announcement of the Saviour.

Still, paradise could no longer be the abode of man. Its delights were not prepared for sinners. By sinning, our first parents had forfeited all the pleasures of the place. No longer could they be permitted to approach the tree of life, of whose fair fruit they had daily partaken. *Life* was insured to them no more. They were under the power of *Death*. God therefore drove them forth from the garden to the toil and pain and tumult of a hostile world:

> "The world was all before them, where to choose
> Their place of rest, and Providence their guide.
> They hand in hand, with wand'ring steps and slow,
> Through Eden took their solitary way."

And they could return no more. Cherubim and a flaming sword that turned every way were placed at the closed and guarded gates of paradise to keep back any bold intruder. Since that fatal fall, no man has trod the walks, rested in the bowers, tasted the fruit, of the sacred garden.

Mournful must have been the thought of the deserted paradise. Melancholy must have been the feelings of the guilty and expelled transgressors as afar they looked upon the towering groves of their former home and remembered with anguish the cause of their banishment.

Wandering back in this brief review to the morning of the world's history, and lingering for a while in the beautiful garden home which was lost by our first parents' disobedience, we are impressed anew with *the excellence of holiness*. That made paradise. Not its salubrious air, not its rich productions, not its exceptional beauty, but the holiness of its dwellers, made it the "garden of delight." As long as they were loyal to God, so long they were blessed, and all things around them were in excellent order, peace, and beautiful harmony. God was their beloved and they were his. Heaven and earth were in delightful accord. Life was rich and full and every way desirable. The lower creatures contributed to their joy and welfare.

Also, we are impressed with the *deplorableness of sin*. One act of disobedience, simple in itself but testing man's regard for God, not only lost paradise for us, but brought on dire calamities of unending nature. It expelled man from the fair home that his Creator had prepared for him, brought on him the curse of God, and sent its sad effects through the whole human history.

> "Earth felt the wound; and Nature from her seat,
> Sighing through all her works, gave signs of woe
> That all was lost."

From that time till now the whole creation groaneth and travaileth in pain, sighing for deliverance from the bondage of corruption. Sorrow, disease, conflict, death, are the heritage of sin here; hereafter to be indignation and wrath, tribulation and anguish, forever.

Sin is transgression of God's law. It is hostile to the glory which belongs to him and to the service which is his due. All holy beings deplore it.

We sometimes wonder that Adam and Eve should have plucked and eaten the forbidden fruit. We make little allowance for their freshness and inexperience. With all the knowledge which we have of sin and its effects, and which they had not, we act as badly as they did. He would be a bold man who should claim that he had not done worse than our first parents. With the disposition which we manifest, and which is universally prevalent, it is wellnigh certain that we would pluck forbidden fruit and bring upon ourselves the judgment of God. It is what we are doing. We perpetuate the sin which Adam originated.

Further, we are impressed with *the necessity and the preciousness of the redemption by Christ*. By his work he has lifted up the curse from our souls. In no other way could it be done. "For as through the one man's disobedience the many were made sinners, even so through the obedience of the one shall the many be made righteous." At the instant of the Fall, God promised that the serpent's head should be bruised. "When the fullness of the time came, God sent forth his Son, born of a woman, born under the law, that he might redeem them which were under the law, that we might receive the adoption of sons." Without that, this world would have been one of despair. Without Christ, the curse would have been perpetual; the ruin of the Fall would have been a helpless ruin. Well, then, may we prize the redemption by our Lord Jesus Christ. Paradise is lost; but paradise may be regained. A brighter home than that which God prepared for man on earth, Christ is preparing for his friends in heaven. Sin spoiled the beauty of the former, and its very site was long since obliterated. But into the latter sin can never enter. There shall be no more curse. And death shall be no more; neither shall there be mourning, nor crying, nor pain, any more; the first things are passed away. The tree of life has been plucked up from the earth; here we cannot find its leaves and its fruit. But it has been transplanted in heaven, where it grows in perennial beauty, bearing twelve manner of fruits, yielding its fruit every month; and the leaves of the tree are for the healing of the nations.

We bid farewell to our lost terrestrial paradise. We shall never drink from its fountains; we shall never gather its peerless flowers; we shall never rest in its bowers. We shall not there walk with God as our first parents walked.

We await the welcome to another paradise.

We pant for its salubrious air; we thirst for the river of the water of life: we hunger for the fruit of the tree of life: we long for the society of just men made perfect: we wait for Christ. Come, Lord Jesus, come quickly!

EPOCH II.

THE ANTEDILUVIAN.

THE ANTEDILUVIAN.

Respecting the long ages from the Fall to the Deluge we know but little. Over nearly all that then transpired and nearly all who then existed rolls the dark wave of oblivion. A few verses of sacred history constitute the only record of more than sixteen centuries of time. Yet the brief statements are full of interest and suggestion of thrilling truth. Those dark days before the flood were days of turbulence and violence and daring crime against God and man. We behold the gigantic forms of wicked men stalking over the earth and blighting it with their slaughter, oppression, and lust. We see righteousness banished from the homes of the world, and at length finding refuge in the bosom of only a single family. Yet during this epoch of blood and sin there were holy men—a goodly succession of those who loved God and who perpetuated the ordinances of religion, whose names the inspired historian has preserved and which shine with brighter splendor on account of the darkness of their times, as brilliant stars at night between enshrouding clouds.

The review and lessons of the antediluvian days bring out a peculiar history. Under the curse of God we have seen our first parents driven forth from paradise to a life of toil and pain. Their natural wants led them at once to settle at some locality where they planted their home and commenced their labors. Their children, brought into the world in pain and anguish, grew up with them and were instructed in the duties of labor and worship. Adam and his wife, although they had so fatally sinned and therefore had suffered, undoubtedly accepted the provisions of grace which God had mercifully announced to them, and lived thenceforth in reconciliation with him. But their repentance could not restore them to that perfect state and that union with God which they had before enjoyed. In paradise there was an intimacy of intercourse with God which they never afterward experienced. There, it was like the intercourse and worship of the angels in heaven. Afterward, God was withdrawn; he appeared to them in visible form no more; he spake with them as friend with friend no more. They brought to him their thank-offerings, and at bloody altars they made sacrifice for sin, of beasts that were slain.

All the world was changed, and all their life

upon it. In paradise the garden produced spontaneously and continuously its undeviating series of fruits for their nourishment. But now the smitten earth required careful cultivation, it produced its harvests reluctantly, and the labor spent upon it was often disappointing. Blight and mildew destroyed the ripening crops. Thorns and thistles sprang up spontaneously over the fields, contending with man for the mastery. Wild beasts became his enemy and ravaged his possessions. Birds of pillage consumed the fruits of his toil and care. Life was a scene of conflict and sweat and hard endurance. What he gained and garnered for his own subsistence was gained by exertion and was truly "the bread of sorrows."

The entire experience of the sinful state was new. Adam was created unconsciously to himself. When Eve was formed, though she was taken from his side, it was as a pleasant dream when one awaketh. But *birth* now had assumed a painful character. Sorrow, pangs next to the limit of endurance, were its accompaniments. It was the distressful reminder to her who was first in transgression, of the evil nature of sin. Mysterious and wonderful to the first parents must have been the birth of their first child, the being of one so helpless, so perfectly formed, so dependent for life, the miniature image of themselves. With mingled emotions of wonder and joy they must have watched the actions, the growth, the development of the bodily and mental powers of their son. It was altogether unlike their own experience. They were made adult, their systems mature and ready for independent life. Here was one entirely dependent upon them, yet daily acquiring strength and approaching maturity. To them was committed the new task of training him for life and duty—in which, perhaps, they failed; for their firstborn brought great calamity upon them by a crime of the darkest character. As they had voluntarily sinned against God, abused his goodness and love, they knew and bore the agony which parents feel from the waywardness and guilt of a beloved child.

The experience of *death* was also new to them. As years passed away, and they, at length, were called to look upon the dead form of one whom they had loved, as they gazed into the rayless eyes once beaming with intelligence, as they laid their hands upon the cold limbs once lithe and active, and heard no voice in response to their call, strange emotions must have overpowered them. Death must have had peculiar terror and they must have shrunk from the dread dissolution of soul and body.

But these facts of birth and death and all the

varied elements of human life came on, and man became accustomed to the experiences of his fallen state. The antediluvian generations multiplied and a strange history was enacted.

One of the most prominent facts is *the extraordinary length of human life* in the days before the flood. We are obliged to recur to what we regard as almost ancient history to ascertain facts no further away than such as the antediluvians might have remembered as occurring in their own lifetime. Adam lived to be nine hundred and thirty years of age; Seth lived nine hundred and twelve years; Jared, nine hundred and sixty-two years; Methuselah, nine hundred and sixty-nine years. Such periods of time would reach back from our day beyond the first crusade to the Holy Land, beyond the days of William the Conqueror, to the founding of Cambridge University; as far back as the time when figures in arithmetic were introduced into Europe by the Saracens; hundreds of years beyond the discovery of America by Columbus. Think of all that has transpired within the past nine hundred and thirty years in the revolutions among the nations, in the progress of learning, science, and religion; and then think that one with a life as long as that of Adam might have witnessed it all.

It is difficult to appreciate such longevity. At

that early period it was permitted for wise reasons. The unoccupied earth was to be peopled, and through such prolonged lives individual families would be greatly increased. It is supposed by some that, for this reason, the earth, during the antediluvian epoch, contained a greater number of inhabitants than it has since done. This longevity would also tend to a great advancement in learning, art, and civilization. The principal reason why greater maturity and perfection are not now attained by men in their various investigations and productions, is that death interrupts their discoveries and stops the studies and inventions which they have pursued. It was not so before the flood. Men then had time to push their investigations, to give system and efficacy to their plans and inventions, and to develop practical results of a mature character. Skill would be matured by such prolonged experiment and that which one thoroughly attained he would have time to communicate to others. We may therefore suppose that the antediluvians approached a state of knowledge and skill, in those works to which their attention was given, such as we should not, at first thought, be apt to impute to those early times. One of the first things mentioned of Cain after his banishment is that he built a city and called it after the name of his son. This would seem to indicate quite a degree of cultivation and knowledge from the earliest times. Of Jubal it is written, " he was the father of all such as handle the harp and organ," showing that the science of music was then cultivated. Tubal-cain is spoken of as "an instructor of every artificer in brass and iron," which indicates the knowledge of architecture, agriculture, and mechanics.

How far the knowledge and attainments and works of the antediluvians extended we are not explicitly informed. We are forced to rely upon inference from the few facts that are stated. We know that Noah, with the knowledge and skill possessed in those days, constructed an ark of more than forty thousand tons burden, which was capable of holding all the varieties of living animals, with food for their sustenance for several months, together with a family of eight persons with supplies for their wants, and which was strong enough to endure the rush and shock of the deluge. We know that not long after the flood the sons of men projected a stupendous tower whose top should reach to heaven, in the building of which they were arrested only by the hand of the Almighty. These things indicate skill and ability to execute corresponding to those of any age. We may therefore suppose that splendid cities and costly towers, princely palaces and capacious edifices for war or for trade, were seen before the flood. Possibly the works of human genius and strength surpassed all that have since been witnessed. The lofty tower of Babel, rising, perhaps, above all the works of man since its day, may be the sole symbol and witness this side of the deluge of what was common before it. The long life of that period would naturally stimulate to the erection of more costly and massive structures than any that have since been attempted.

How far, in other respects, the achievements of art, science, and skill were carried must be left to conjecture, aided only by the slightest hints from the brief Scripture narrative. The prolonged life of the antediluvians certainly gave them peculiar advantages for attaining distinction and perfection in every work to which they gave devoted attention.

Moreover, we know that the East, the land of Noah, has from the earliest times been the seat and source of science and art. There flourished the powerful empires of the ancient world. There stood the splendid cities whose disentombed ruins now astonish excavators and explorers. There sculpture and the kindred arts were carried to a high degree of perfection. There astronomy had its post-diluvian birth. There arithmetic was studied, and the science of numbers came thence to the western lands. There are found the lithographic monuments which are yielding new light from age to age on the facts of most ancient history. From these lands have flowed forth the streams of knowledge and taste and power which have blessed the nations of the world. Who shall say that all that Babylon and Nineveh accomplished, all that the human mind in the wide range of its achievements in Egypt and Arabia and among other peoples of the Orient attained, was anything more than the relics of what the world had witnessed in the days of its antediluvian vigor and glory?

The uniformity of human language is another striking characteristic of this epoch. By this common bond the human family was held together. We see the strength of that bond now. A common language bespeaks brotherhood. A strange tongue implies separation. Language is that which characterizes peoples. In those days wherever men went they found their own dialect universally spoken. A common language would lead to common aims and attainments and to a universal advancement. Great undertakings would be carried forward with higher hopes of success than could otherwise be expected. It is in the prophecies of future greatness and glory that the nations shall come back to the possession and use of a common language. When God purposed to bring human counsels to nought and put an end to the gigantic works which men had impiously undertaken, he confounded their language. Since then, nations, however numerous and powerful, may not have been able to accomplish what before a united world could accomplish.

We know but little of the customs of society, the manner of life, and the forms of government among the antediluvians. Marriage has been known from the beginning, an institution of God coeval with the race. The family and the home have therefore always existed. A son of Cain first practiced polygamy, then, as always, contrary to the ordinance of God, a human abuse of a divine regulation. The Sabbath was an established ordinance of God. Worship, in some form, was more or less practiced. Families were probably united for the promotion of common interests; while powerful clans arose as events advanced. Over all human institutions was the manifest control of God.

But the most striking characteristic of the antediluvian epoch was *its extraordinary and terrible wickedness.* That was the iron age of crime. Men toiled in sin and debasement. They rioted in lust and blasphemy. The very earth reeled under the tramp and rush of its maddened and turbulent population. Before the frantic onset of vice everything good and hallowed was swept away. "There were giants in those days," men who were monsters of oppression, lust, and crime. Wickedness attained a gigantic growth: "Every imagination of the thoughts of man's heart was only evil continually. The earth was corrupt before God, and the earth was filled with violence. And it repented the Lord that he had made man on the earth, and it grieved him at his heart." Crime had an early beginning. Hardly had the first family become settled when their first-born child reddened his hands with his brother's blood. Wicked and envious Cain lifted his hand against the gentle and pious Abel, so covering his name with everlasting infamy as the first murderer. The weeping parents bowed over the cold form of their martyred son, whose spirit was the first to ascend from earth to heaven, and they were pierced anew with sorrow over the bitter fruits of their sin in paradise. Cain was cursed, and he went forth a fugitive and a vagabond in the earth. In the land of Nod he founded a wicked state where infidelity and vice prevailed. This, perhaps, became the fountain head of those temptations which assailed the sons of God and which brought on a deep and dreadful degeneracy and corruption. For a time the descendants of the pious patriarchs, Seth, Enos and others, remained distinct and continued the ordinances of religion; but, as the race multiplied, they became acquainted with those of an opposite character, and, breaking away from the restraints of education and habit, " the sons of God " formed unhallowed alliances with " the daughters of men." " They took them wives of all that they chose." The result was a profligate progeny, a race of gigantic sinners. From that time the wickedness of man was great in the earth.

There were, indeed, some who loved and served God. In the fifth chapter of Genesis a genealogy is given probably of those who were pious, the line of holy men who, amid the prevailing wickedness, maintained the worship of God. Among these was Enoch, who " walked with God," and " was translated that he should not see death," and who " before his translation had witness borne to him that he had been well-pleasing unto God." Among the depraved of his day he stood forth in faithful testimony for the truth, rebuking sinners by his pure life and his solemn warnings. Like Elijah, he was borne away from the earth, a witness of the immortality of man, of the reality of the future life. " He was not; for God took him." But although the generation of the pious was continued, yet goodness rapidly diminished and there was an alarming increase of wickedness. Commencing in families, corruption extended through all ranks of social and civil life. Religion and its claims were banished from their minds. Violence reigned. There was oppression, robbery, and bold murder. The strong plundered the weak and every man's hand was set against his fellow.

We can form but a faint idea of the world in that epoch of licentiousness and crime. So polluted and debased had men become, that Jehovah repented that he had made them, and he determined by one tremendous deluge to sweep them and all the marks and monuments of their sin from the face of the earth. One man alone found favor with God, the righteous Noah, whose faith in God never faltered, and who, when men went mad in sin, maintained unswerving loyalty to his Maker. To him God communicated his purpose to destroy the world, and he commanded him to build an ark sufficiently large to hold his family and all the species of living animals. One of the most sublime declarations in human annals is that respecting Noah's obedience: "Thus did Noah; according to all that God commanded him, so did he."

The strong timbers of that famous and stupendous structure were laid. Its architect was God. We can faintly imagine the merriment and ribaldry and scorn which such a work must have caused. The impious and profane would certainly mock the old man, who, with the frosts of five centuries upon his head, had undertaken to build such an immense vessel in anticipation of a flood which was to come at the end of one hundred and twenty years. But the venerable patriarch did not pause in his labor. He believed God, and no taunts of the wicked could move him. All things moved forward as they had done. The seasons came and went and years passed away. The violence of man knew no pause, and lust and carnage waxed more intense. Noah continued his work, and as a "preacher of righteousness" admonished guilty men to repent before the fearful doom should come upon them. But no man heeded his message. Sunken in sensuality, given over to hardness of heart and debasement of life, they rushed on recklessly in their career to ruin.

At length the ark was completed. It was stored with provisions. Noah and his family entered it; and, after them, from the four quarters of the globe and the heavens, came the living animals, two by two, and took their appointed places in peace in the vast fabric provided for their accommodation. A feeling of awe must have passed through the minds of the world's guilty and reckless population as they saw the air darkened by the flying birds which swept into the ark, and as they beheld the beasts of the field and of the forest, the gentle and ferocious, in one magnificent procession, defiling into the ponderous structure with order and harmony. The ark was filled; its door was shut; God became the protector of its inmates.

Seven days still passed by, and all things continued as they were. Men gazed upon the closed and guarded edifice, and then plunged into their sins. All was tumult and crime and wilder gayety than ever. "They ate, they drank, they married, they were given in marriage, until the day that Noah entered the ark, and the flood came, and destroyed them all."

At last there came a night of darkness. Heavy clouds piled their dense masses upon masses, and pealing thunder shook the foundations of the solid globe. Forked and glaring lightning blazed over the earth, succeeded by a deeper darkness than before. Sleep forsook every eyelid, and every man's heart quaked for fear. In gloom and alarm they waited through that long night for the morning. But no morning rose upon them. The hour for the day introduced a wilder tumult of the elements than the night had known. Peal followed peal until it seemed that the heavens were shattered. Crash succeeded crash until the earth seemed to be rent asunder. Then came the deluge. "The same day were all the fountains of the great deep broken up, and the windows of heaven were opened." Torrents, huge volumes of water, descended from above; while from their deep bed the waters of the ocean rose and rolled in overwhelming violence across the earth. They shook the mountains as they dashed against them, and the white spray was hurled over their towering crests. Human habitations were whelmed by the advancing flood. Towns and cities and all the massive works of art and skill disappeared, like grain before the sickle of the reaper. Beasts and every living thing sunk under the engulfing waves. The fowls of heaven were dashed with stunning force to the earth. Onward rolled the surging waters. The ancient forests fell before them. The wrecks and ruins of proud empires were borne afar. "And every living substance was destroyed which was upon the face of the ground, both man, and cattle, and the creeping things, and the fowl of the heaven: and they were destroyed from the earth; and Noah only remained alive, and they that were with him in the ark." A globe of water swung through the heavens, with only one dark, moving substance upon it, the solitary ark of the patriarch, conveying the sole survivors of the old world to be the pioneers of the new world.

Thus has the second scene in the world's great drama passed before us, with its warning and instruction. It reads to us the solemn lesson that *all men must die*. Great was the age of the antediluvians; but the history of each one closes with the comprehensive and personal phrase, "And he died." "All the days that Adam lived were nine hundred and thirty years: and he died." He lived to witness the dire effects of his sin and to mourn in bitterness for it. He saw nine generations of his children peopling the smitten earth, and he saw how from one sin a race became corrupt. Methuselah lived nine hundred and sixty-nine years; and he died. "Yea, though a man live a thousand years twice told, yet hath he seen no good: do not all go to one place?" "It is appointed unto men once to die."

We learn also that *human nature, when unrestrained, is prone to excesses in sin*. What a scene of depravity is given in the history of the antediluvian world! A whole race, with few exceptions, was given up to wildest lusts and crimes. At last, one man alone remained faithful to God.

"God saw that the wickedness of man was great in the earth, and that every imagination of the thoughts of his heart was only evil continually." Thus it is with man unrestrained. His tendency is downward. He is of the earth, earthy. Nor is he satisfied with being earthy; he must grovel. Sin leads on to excess. It corrupted man so that God repented that he had made him. It was because the world was deluged with sin that it had to be deluged with water.

Again, we learn from the fate of the antediluvians that *God regards sin with abhorrence.* It was then terribly expressed. It was expressed when he drove man out of paradise and guarded its gates with the flaming cherubim; when he cursed the sinners and cursed the earth that they trod upon. But it was more impressively expressed when he sunk the whole world under the flood. Six generations of living men thronged the earth with a mighty population. Two thousand years had accumulated great works of genius, power and art. Populous cities, with their strong walls and palaces, had sprung into being. All over the world were cultivated fields, homes of men, millions of hearts full of life and hope. But it mattered not; God could not put up with their aggravated sins, he abhorred those workers of iniquity. So he opened the windows of heaven, and broke up the fountains of the great deep, and with a wild and universal deluge swept them all away. He cleansed the earth of its wickedness. He whelmed in one promiscuous and awful ruin the race of man and its works. The marks of that fearful flood, in the scarred rocks, in the changes on the surface of the globe, are so many enduring memorials of God's abhorrence of sin.

Lastly, we are reminded of *God's faithfulness to his friends.* Amid the prevalent wickedness, he did not overlook that one man of prayer who alone maintained religion on the earth. He foretold him of the flood and taught him to prepare for it. For one hundred and twenty years, amid the taunts of men, God upheld him and gave him unwavering confidence in the promise. When the ark was finished, and the aged patriarch had retired within it, God shut him in and guarded him from the assaults of the wicked who during the seven days of suspense hung around it. God was with him during the fearful days of the deluge. His hand guided the mighty fabric as it floated over the sunken world, with its precious freight, the sole surviving relic of the antediluvian days. God is ever faithful to his friends.

Here we bid adieu to our earth as it first existed. We look out on the shoreless sea where once were the homes and works of a multitudinous population. Will the world remain forever whelmed, or will it appear again from those overflowing floods?

EPOCH III.

THE PATRIARCHAL.

THE PATRIARCHAL.

LIKE the calm on the sea when the rage of the tempest has died away, like the hush on the fields when the storm has spent its fury, is the gentle patriarchal epoch after the turbulent antediluvian days. Conflict, oppression, violence, and vice, are succeeded by peace, order, and paternal rule. We look upon scenes of gentleness and rural beauty. We see feeding flocks and herds tended by faithful servants, scattered over the verdant meadows and by the crystal streams. We behold the white pavilions of the patriarchs pitched by the borders of shadowing groves, while near them are the humbler tents of their retainers. It is the mild pastoral age, an age, however, of checkered events and not without its stirring annals.

After a year's confinement in the ark, Noah and his family and all the animals went forth to inhabit again the world that had been deluged. The vestiges of the former earth had disappeared. Its mighty population, its works of skill and grandeur, its cultivated fields, its towns and cities, all had utterly perished. Naught remained but the bare mountains and the broad territory torn and scarred by the rushing flood. They went forth, those few survivors, with wonder and gratitude, again to possess and people the renovated earth. The aged patriarch at once reared an altar, and the prayer of thanksgiving ascended with the smoke of sacrifice. God was pleased with the offering, and immediately vouchsafed gracious promises to Noah and his sons, conferred upon them higher prerogatives than he had before conferred upon Adam, and entered into holy covenant with them. The bow on the clouds, overarching the earth, became the signet and memorial, from that time, through every age, of the faithfulness of God. The joyous seasons returned again, traversing the world with their perpetual round of blessing, the varied gifts and bounties of Providence, hymning in every zone their harmonic and delightful chorus. Verdure again clothed the drenched earth, and the hills and valleys smiled with their antediluvian beauty. The beasts and birds departed to the places that were suited to their nature, subject to the dominion and impressed with the awe of man. The patriarch and his sons, invested with supreme lordship over the world, inspired by the promises of their Maker and by the rapid progress in the vegetable world, engaged in the labors and duties of life. They reared their habitations, planted vineyards, tended their flocks and herds, and gradually established the manners and institutions of a new civilization. Their descendants spread abroad, and by degrees the earth was peopled anew. The old patriarch, who had lived six centuries before the flood, lived three hundred and fifty years after it, and so attained a greater age than that of any other man since that remarkable event. From that time the period of human life was greatly shortened.

For many years after the deluge the form and customs of society were simple. Noah, for whose sake God had preserved alive the few survivors of the ancient world, was doubtless revered by his descendants, who paid high respect to his authority and instruction. His sons, Shem, Ham and Japheth, whose posterity respectively inhabited Asia, Africa and Europe, also exercised patriarchal authority; and for a while the institutions of society and the arts of life prosperously advanced.

But alas! scenes of sin and tumult appeared, blighting the promise of the new world. The earth does not seem to be the native clime of virtue and religion. Even the flood did not permanently cleanse and purify it. The severe lessons of that great calamity were forgotten or disregarded even within the lifetime of Noah. His great-grandson followed the example of the antediluvian giants, broke away from the patriarchal rule, and assumed unlawful and violent authority. He is represented as "a mighty hunter before the Lord." He was a bold hunter of men, a strong and reckless oppressor. He gathered to himself wild and lawless spirits and assaulted and subjugated others. He set up his own authority as supreme, and he became a daring usurper and tyrant. Under his leadership, probably, the project was formed of erecting on the plain of Shinar "a city, and a tower whose top should reach unto heaven." The object of this bold design was to create an important metropolis which should be the center of power and influence, the capital of the world.

Nimrod was probably moved to the undertaking by a desire to consolidate his power and to gratify his pride. The tower was to be his fortress, and from that stronghold he intended to march forth on a career of conquest and dominion. His followers desired to accomplish something which would render them illustrious; and all who engaged in the enterprise supposed that it would tend to prevent the inhabitants of the world from being "scattered abroad upon the face of the whole earth." As this design became known, we can imagine that people, near and far, thronged to the rising city and joined in the building of the lofty tower. Multitudes of workmen swarmed over the fields, preparing the bricks and cement, and other multitudes bore them to the artizans who were erecting the walls. So the gigantic undertaking went forward, story rising above story, until indeed it seemed to aspire to heaven. It was all displeasing to God. It was planned with no reference to his desire and was in distinct opposition to his purpose. "Man proposes; God disposes." By the exercise of his power he brought the whole thing to naught. He touched the lips of the builders and confused their language, "so that they could not understand one another's speech." This confusion of tongues confused their plans and labors. One could not comprehend what another wanted. At once, and of necessity, they ceased the building and were scattered abroad over the world. Thus God turned the counsels of the impious men against themselves and secured the very result against which they conspired. We hear no more of the arrogant hunter. The clamor caused by the miraculous confusion of tongues gave that tower a name which it has borne ever since: the tower of Babel. Its riven and blasted pile stands in ruin on the sterile plain of Babylonia, a monument of the folly of man and of the divine retribution.

This dispersion of the human family, while it was necessary for its growth and sustenance and also that the broad territories of the earth might be peopled and cultivated, seems to have produced an unfortunate effect as to their spiritual interests. As men retreated from the sacred places of antiquity, they seemed to forget the lessons of the past, to forget their relation to God. Idolatry, in various forms, assumed the place of true worship, until the religion of the earliest patriarchs was threatened with extermination. The pastoral life led men to observe and reflect upon the objects and powers of nature; and as faith in God died out of their minds, very naturally they came to deify and adore the invisible power, or the object in which divinity apparently resided. Hence the hosts of heaven were worshiped; temples and altars were built to the sun, moon, and stars, and from consecrated places incense arose to the celestial orbs. A lower grade of idolatry consisted in the worship of man-made images, to which a degeneracy of manners and character directly led.

In order that his name and worship might be honored and perpetuated, God determined to call forth Abraham, a godly man, from all others, and to make of him a mighty nation which amid the prevailing idolatries should maintain true religion in the world. This call introduces us to a new chapter in patriarchal history. A succession of eminent men appeared, whose names are the most distinguished in the world's annals: Abraham, Isaac, Jacob, the fathers of the Hebrew nationality, the founders of the Hebrew theocracy. Their names and their influence coexist with the race, being honored by Jew, Christian, and Mohammedan. Foremost of these is Abraham, whose name is reverenced in many lands, who is claimed as the patriarch of various religious dynasties, who is beloved as the head of "the chosen people," the prince of the great Hebrew commonwealth; who has been, and is yet to be more widely, reverenced as the "Father of the faithful" among Jews and Gentiles, who, in every land, shall become partakers of his faith. Israel, "a name divinely blest," recalls hallowed memories of the Church through successive ages, when they who have been "Israelites indeed" have borne testimony to their faith, while it carries us forward to the time when, with "the whole Israel of God," we shall stand on the Mount Zion above.

We turn with pleasure to the artless story of the patriarchal times. Those faithful men were not without their frailties and faults. The sacred narrative does not represent them as demigods, nor yet men of perfect character or life. It sets them before us as those who loved God and who were kept by him, and needed to be kept, in the way of righteousness. Their life was a simple one, the life of wandering shepherds, yet it was a life of independence and nobility.

They were *Fathers*, exercising paternal authority and watchfulness over their great households, regulating the domestic and social customs of all, and consulted freely by every individual under their care.

They were *Priests*, presiding over and leading in the worship of God, appointing the sacred festivals, and offering for all the accustomed sacrifices.

They were *Chiefs*, supreme in their rule, maintaining justice and punishing wickedness, training their servants for the duties of war and going forth at their head to battle, forming alliances with kings and surrounding patriarchs, and exercising with undisputed right the prerogatives of sovereignty. Opulent in their extensive herds and flocks, their treasures and servants, they preserved their freedom and were able to repel acts of violence. They were not merely men of uncultivated manners and rude but generous bearing; but with their generosity there was united a politeness and a magnanimity which made them the compeers of kings who lived in palaces. They were characterized by bravery and piety, and were respected or feared by those who had acquaintance and intercourse with them. In their trembling tents the law of God was reverenced, and by their builded altars they recognized his authority and their obligations.

They were *heroes*, not in the diminutive, worldly sense, not by the superiority of brute force, but by a higher and holier calling—their walk with God. Theirs was the heroism of faith; a heroism celebrated by the inspired writer in a roll-call of the heroes, two thousand years after their time, and which has animated the people of God in every age. They looked upon themselves as pilgrims and strangers upon earth. While sojourning in a land not their own and dwelling in tents, they looked for the city which hath the foundations, whose builder and maker is God. They lived as in the constant presence of God; their footsteps were guided by his hand, and holy angels encamped round about them. On every hand the world was becoming polluted with wickedness and the rites of a profane idolatry; but the soil which they occupied was sacred to God, and in their tabernacles was preserved the early faith and the primitive worship. In whatever relation of life we behold them, the Hebrew patriarchs have a character unique and interesting. There is the same simplicity of manners, the same regard for the rights and welfare of others, the same subdued heroism, the same reverence for God. Wandering over the plains of Canaan, sojourning in the capitals of kings, abiding at their rural residences, they still bear the same lineaments and stand forth peculiar and venerable among those who surround them.

Illustrations of their character, and of the divine love for them, abound in the sacred history of their lives. At the call of God, Abraham forsook home and kindred and native land, the associations of his youth and manhood and the graves of his fathers, and went forth into a strange land, "not knowing whither he went." Relying implicity oh the Being who summoned him, he knew no discouragement and his faith did not falter. However strange his course may have seemed to others, however dark the prospect may have been to himself, he pressed on in the might and confidence of one who honored the commission of God. His fidelity was rewarded by glorious promises: "In thee shall all the families of the earth be blessed. I will establish my covenant between me and thee and thy seed after thee in their generations for an everlasting covenant, to be a God unto thee, and to thy seed after thee."

The valor and magnanimity of the patriarch are seen in the incident recorded in the fourteenth chapter of Genesis. Some of the wild chiefs of the country, like the Kurds of our day, had made a predatory incursion into the land of Canaan, and were returning with their plunder, when they were met by the kings of the plain, whom they defeated; whereupon they pillaged Sodom and Gomorrah and carried away Lot and his family as prisoners. A man who escaped bore the tidings to the Hebrew patriarch, who quickly armed his trained men and pursued the marauders. He fell upon them by night and completely routed them, recovering their booty and delivering his kinsman and family. On his return he met the illustrious Melchizedek, to whom he gave tithes and by whom he was blessed. Melchizedek was the king of Salem and was also priest of his people, and, like Abraham, he had preserved the knowledge and worship of the true God. Further than this his history is unknown; and it is this fact which led the apostle to speak of him as "without father, without mother, without genealogy, having neither beginning of days nor end of life." Abraham also refused to retain any portion of the recovered property, so showing that it was only from motives of humanity that he became a warrior.

Another scene of interest is laid at Mamre. It was the sultry hour of noon when the patriarch sat at his tent-door, looking out at his grazing herds and indulging in devout reflection. Three men appeared before him, whom he greeted and entertained with gracious patriarchal hospitality. One of these august visitors revealed himself to Abraham as a divine person and announced to him the speedy fulfillment of a precious promise. He also declared to that "friend of God" the purpose of his coming to the earth at that time—the investigation of the wickedness of Sodom and Gomorrah. The sympathies of the patriarch were roused by the announcement. He knew the guilt of those cities, and he feared for their fate, especially for his friends who were residing there. He made an intercession in their behalf, perhaps the most touching, affectionate, confiding, prevalent, in all the history of human prayer; revealing, on the one hand, the condescension and mercy of God, and on the other hand, the tenderness and the might of the humble supplicant. With characteristic devotion and faith, that holy man stood between the offending cities and their offended Monarch, and by the power of intercession reduced the number from fifty to ten for whose sake, if they could be found in those cities, God promised to spare them. But ten righteous persons could not be found in Sodom and Gomorrah, and those cities were doomed.

On the next morning, Abraham went to the place where he had stood before the Lord, and there he beheld a sight which baffled description. Sodom and Gomorrah were wrapped in sheets of devouring flame. Out of heaven the Lord rained brimstone and fire upon them; and the people and all the buildings of those cities and the plain on which they stood were consumed in the terrible conflagration, the smoke of which rolled up like the smoke of a mighty furnace.

The patriarch bowed in holy fear and submission before the Lord his God. Afterward came the memorable trial of his faith. Unexpectedly, when he was enjoying the prospect of a calm old age, with the son who had been given to him in fulfillment of the promise, he received a command from God to take that son, and to sacrifice him as a burnt offering on a mountain of Moriah. Startling, dreadful, as the command must have been, Abraham obeyed. Early in the morning, he set out on the mournful journey to Moriah. The parting of Isaac that morning with his mother, the unconsciousness of the youth, must have nearly broken the heart of the old man. But he knew in whom he believed. His soul was stayed upon the Almighty. For three days they journeyed to the mountain. Leaving the servants at the foot, the father and the son toiled up the rugged ascent, Isaac bearing the wood, Abraham the fire and the knife. Suddenly, Isaac spake: "My father, behold the fire and the wood; but where is the lamb for a burnt offering?" "My son," replied the smitten father, "God will provide himself a lamb for a burnt offering." Reaching the appointed place, the altar was built, the wood was laid in order upon it, and Isaac was bound and placed upon the wood, and then the father raised aloft the knife for the fatal blow. The startling voice of God, speaking in that lonely place and forbidding the sacrifice, alone arrested the uplifted arm, and the gleaming blade fell ringing by the altar. The wonderful faith of the patriarch was fully tested, and from that time he became the acknowledged "Father of the faithful." Additional divine blessings were then pronounced upon him.

Not long after this Sarah died, and Abraham buried her in the cave of the field of Machpelah, which he purchased, in the manner of a prince, from the sons of Heth. There, when he came to die, "in a good old age, an old man, and full of years," the patriarch himself was buried. In the simple manner of the patriarchal age, Isaac lived, a man of gentle and unobtrusive character, and, in advanced life, was "gathered unto his people," and buried in the same cave of Machpelah. There too, after a life of romantic interest, with mournful ceremonies, the embalmed body of the patriarch Jacob was deposited by his weeping sons.

Of the lives of the twelve patriarchs, the heads of the great tribes of Israel, that of Joseph is by far the most interesting, possessing the mingled charm of fiction and truth of history, and depicting in most artless language the working of divine providence. A succession of fascinating and thrilling scenes passes before us. An upright youth is torn from a tender father by fraternal violence; a captive slave in a strange land, he is thrust unjustly into prison; he becomes the acting head of a populous and powerful empire, swaying its destinies with prophetic wisdom and bringing about a social revolution unmatched in historic annals. The brethren who sold him into Egypt, by stress of famine bow before him; a mutual recognition takes place, and the whole patriarchal family makes a settlement in a part of the Egyptian realm. Peaceful and honored was the death of the noble and gentle Joseph, mourned alike by Hebrew and Egyptian.

Here we take our leave of the peculiar patriarchal epoch and of that succession of distinguished names which illustrated and graced it. It has left to us its lessons of warning and instruction.

The daring *career of Nimrod* shows us how slow men are to profit by the judgments of the past. The marks of the flood were not effaced before he renewed the wickedness of the antediluvian times.

The fate of *Babel's builders* shows us how God can turn the plans of wicked men against themselves, and from their temporary success secure his wise and permanent designs.

The results of selfishness are set forth in the *history of Lot.* He chose the rich plains of Sodom for his pasture-grounds when Abraham generously offered him his choice; he pitched his own tent toward Sodom, and he wellnigh perished in the terrible ruin of the place. Idolaters and proud foes of Israel, children of incest, were his only descendants.

The triumphs and blessings of faith are strikingly manifested in the noble life of *the patriarch Abraham.* Revered by the faithful of every age, his name is the symbol and representative of unswerving confidence in God. In the everlasting covenant which Jehovah made with him, we and our children share, with all who by faith are the children of faithful Abraham. In the life of *Jacob* we see the sad effects of sin. His deception of his father and betrayal of his brother led to a lifetime of disorder. The example of *Joseph* on the other hand, presents the beauty of youthful piety and the blessings which it secures in after life.

EPOCH IV.

THE MOSAIC.

THE MOSAIC.

The Hebrew commonwealth was of a peculiar character. Whether we look at its founder, its origin, its object, its duration, or its results, it stands forth grand and unique among the dominions of the world. Commencing fifteen centuries before the Christian era, it saw empire after empire rise and fall and disappear, while still it held on its course, swaying the minds of a powerful people by its authority, and impressing many nations by its religion and its laws. And now, although long ago its capital and glory and its renowned institutions were lost; although its judges and the proud line of its kings exist no more; and although the voices of its rapt prophets are hushed, its power and influence live with that peculiar people who maintain the Hebrew character and faith. Scattered and peeled, driven forth from the goodly heritage of their fathers, oppressed in every land and become a byword and reproach, they have still remained distinct, perpetuating the characteristic features, the religious rites, and the national traits of their early ancestry. Though many times conquered, they have not been exterminated; though carried as captives into strange lands, they have never mingled with their captors—the blood of the patriarchs flows uncontaminated in their veins. Few, comparatively, are the children of the promise who now inhabit the promised land; their songs are silent on Zion's sacred hill; the Moslem mosque sacrilegiously crowns the polluted summit of Moriah. Of late, increased attention has been directed to Palestine as the predicted home of the Jewish people, and thousands of emigrants have secured land and built their dwellings within sight of sacred Jerusalem; while from the four quarters of the globe the dispersed children of Israel are looking thither in anticipation of the renewal of the ancient glory and the restored inheritance of their race.

The land of Canaan was early given to the patriarch Abraham and his descendants by the purpose and promise of God. Hard necessity led Jacob and his sons to sojourn in Egypt, where Joseph was then the prime minister of state. But it was only for a season. In Egypt they increased so rapidly that they roused the jealousy of the government. The illustrious services of Joseph were forgotten, and the promises of protection to his people, which a former Pharaoh had made, were disregarded. A system of repression was adopted which was designed to crush the spirit and check the growth of the Israelites and to make them slaves of the Egyptians. From their freedom as shepherds they were reduced to a degrading vassalage. Exacting task-masters were appointed over them, and menial service was assigned to them—the digging of clay, the making of bricks, the bearing of burdens for their haughty oppressors. "But the more they afflicted them, the more they multiplied and the more they spread abroad." Baffled and enraged, the wicked monarch formed a murderous scheme for the destruction of all the infant sons of the Hebrews. His edict was overruled by an all-directing Providence for the ruin of the Egyptians and the emancipation of the children of Israel.

As the daughter of Pharaoh, with her attendant maidens, walked by the banks of the Nile, she saw, floating among the flags, a little ark, which she opened, and, "Behold! a male infant, weeping." Touched by the crying and by the beauty of the child, the princess determined to adopt him as her own and to educate him as her son and heir. So Moses became, in after years, the leader and lawgiver of his own people.

Egypt had become to them what it was afterward called in their history and poetry, "the house of bondage." Year after year their infant sons were cast into the Nile; year after year they were worn and wasted by their rigorous servitude. Yet the people became attached to that land, and often, after their exodus, they were found sighing to return to it. To the unsophisticated Hebrews there was something captivating and impressive in the proud monarchy, the gorgeous religion, the learning and art, of the Egyptians. The civil and religious institutions to which they were introduced were in sharp contrast with the simplicity and piety of the patriarchal methods. From their pastoral life on the peaceful plains of Canaan they were brought to a land of palaces and temples and pyramids, the land most advanced in civilization and science. Yet Egypt was not their home-land; they were destined to return to the land of their fathers, the land of promise.

Three qualifications were requisite in one who should successfully lead the Hebrews forth from the country where they had suffered, but for which they had a strong attachment, to their covenanted inheritance in Canaan.

He must, in the first place, be a Hebrew, loving the God of the patriarchs, and devoted to the Hebrew faith. The people had to a great extent swung away from the religion of their fathers, and there was need of a pious and controlling mind to bring them back to their lost worship.

In the second place, he must be an Egyptian, well acquainted with the institutions which had captivated the Hebrew mind, and able to construct a system which, on the one hand, should not inflame their prejudices, and, on the other hand, should readily secure their return and loyalty to Jehovah. Their residence for hundreds of years among a people in many respects their superiors had caused them to become thoroughly Egyptianized, and no one but an Egyptian could have led them from practices of idolatry to the true worship of God.

In the third place, it was requisite that their leader should be acquainted with the life of the desert, so that he could guide and rule the people during their future wanderings of forty years.

By marvelous providences Moses became eminently qualified for this station and mission. Nursed, at the request of the royal princess, by his own Hebrew mother, and trained during his earlier years in a pious Hebrew family, his first and strongest sympathies and principles were with the people of God and their faith. He bore upon his person the sacramental symbol of a holy covenant relation with the God of his fathers. No instruction of after years, no influences nor temptations which environed him, even in the palace of the king and the manners of the court, could ever erase from his mind the impressions and truths which he received in the home of his childhood and from a tender mother's lips.

Adopted by the daughter of Egypt's monarch and furnished with every advantage of his high position, taught by the wisest instructors of the realm, and fitted to become the successor of the Pharaohs, he was learned in all the wisdom of the Egyptians and was skilled in political and religious science. His intellectual mind led him to the foremost rank among the young scholars of Egypt, while his connection with the royal family gave him commanding influence with his associates. It is said that he held a high position in the national armies and as a military leader gained distinguished successes. Familiar with the entire structure of the Egyptian system, he became pre-eminently qualified for the mission to which he was assigned among his people. But this was not all. Burning with strong desire for the deliverance of his race from their wretched servitude, he longed to stand forth in their behalf and with his own arm strike for their freedom. But the time had not come. Stung by the indignities offered to his brethren, he on one occasion passionately resented the wrong, and then fled from Egypt.

In the wilderness of Midian, among a people allied to the Israelites and who still preserved the knowledge and worship of the true God, in the quiet occupation of a shepherd, he received a training in strong contrast with that which he had received in the home of his parents or at the court of Pharaoh, but not less necessary. In the solitudes of nature, the illustrious exile from the pleasures and emoluments of the Egyptian capital, was brought into communion with God and the contemplation of divine truth. Along the base of Sinai and Horeb he led his wandering flocks, where in coming years he was to lead the great hosts of Israel. Here he experienced a discipline which prepared him for the duties and trials of the wonderful career to which he was destined. There is not a life in sacred or profane history of such thrilling interest, leading through scenes of such magnificent and solemn character, as the life of Israel's greatest man. From his rescue when an infant by the royal princess, through his early education, his brilliant manhood, his lofty station as the vicegerent of God, the sublime transactions in which he had the most important part, on to his lonely death and his unknown burial, there is the interest of history, the pathos of endurance, and the wonder of miracle. As we contemplate his character we are conscious of the presence of a superior man—one of the noblest and most honored in human annals. He has boldness, chastened and subdued; diffidence that needs divine encouragement; faith that never falters; jealousy for God and the divine law, untiring energy, meekness that characterizes the man. His life is a triumph. It stands apart from all others—grander, nearer to God.

In the lonely desert, God spake to him from the burning bush that was not consumed, declaring the divine sympathy for the suffering children of Israel and commissioning Moses as their deliverer. He and his brother Aaron were warmly welcomed by the elders of the people, and they entered with confidence on their mission. But their appeal to Pharaoh was spurned; God was despised, and the oppression of the people was increased. Then came the plagues. Sweeping over the doomed land, one after another, ten successive and fearful scourges revealed the power and vengeance of the Hebrews' God. Continuously increasing in intensity and virulence, they laid waste the kingdom and ruined the hopes and the works of its people. The Nile, their chief divinity, was turned into blood, bearing death on its pestilential floods. Life became full of misery and insupportable. Their cattle were swept away; the products of the field were destroyed; their persons were consumed with burning inflictions; light was altogether withdrawn from them, and their dwellings were in darkness that could be felt. Last and direst of all, came the plague of death, when the firstborn of every family in Egypt was destroyed. In every dwelling the cry of the dying startled all the people, from the palace of Pharaoh down to the lowest habitation; a wail of common anguish went up from the whole afflicted nation. On that midnight the haughty king relented. On that midnight six hundred thousand strong men, גְּבָרִים, closed around the families of Jacob, as in order and with rejoicing they moved forth from the land of their oppressors, where for two hundred and fifteen years they had sojourned, "and there was not one feeble person among all their tribes." With a high hand did the Lord lead them out, going before them in a pillar of cloud by day and a pillar of fire by night.

At the end of three days, Pharaoh repented that he had allowed the Israelites to escape, and at the head of his swarthy warriors he pursued them. To the Hebrews it might well have seemed that all was lost. Behind them were the mailed warriors and the armed chariots of their enemy. Before them was the impassable sea, while on either side rose frowning mountains. The courage and faith of Moses rose to the occasion. He quieted the murmurs of the frightened people. He calmly received from God the command, "Speak unto the children of Israel, that they go forward." Then the pillar of the cloud and fire, which had gone before them, moved in silent majesty to their rear, shedding its brilliant light during that long night upon the wakeful Israelites and frowning in blackness upon the bewildered armies of Egypt. Moses stretched forth his rod over the sea, and through its parted floods a dry pathway was formed for the passage of the millions of Israel. When the morning dawned, the waters had resumed their usual appearance. On the farther shore stood the triumphant people of God, while far and wide on the angry waves floated the wreck of Egypt's pride and power—banners that had flaunted in the breeze of yesterday, weapons that had flashed in its light, chariots and horses of war, bodies of armed men, nobles of the realm, and the crowned king, all whelmed in the dreadful overthrow. Mingled with the anthem of the sea, rose the hallelujahs of Israel's hosts, Moses and Miriam leading their psalm of victory and praise.

It was a long and weary discipline through which the Hebrews were compelled to pass before their decimated hosts were permitted to enter the promised land. Accustomed to the debasing influence of idolatrous Egypt, they were slow to yield to the authority of Jehovah, and so stubborn were they that the Almighty determined that none of those who were adult at the exodus from Egypt should enter the land of Canaan. For forty years therefore they wandered through the desert, until they were all buried beneath its soil. For forty years God rained manna from heaven around the camps of Israel for the sustenance of the people. For forty years he passed before them in the pillar of cloud by day and fire by night, piloting their course through a country unknown by them. It was a long, hard training that the nation endured through those forty years. By impressive manifestations, the law was given at Mount Sinai. The tents of Israel were pitched near its base, when suddenly a cloud descended and rested upon its summit, from which lightning flashed and thunder pealed. Silence and awe held the watching multitude. Then came the clear, piercing note of a trumpet, waxing louder and louder, until the mountain quaked and the people trembled. By a still, small voice, soft as a whisper but clear as a clarion, Moses was summoned to the presence of God; and then the law was announced—the divine code which was to be supreme in Israel and which was to be authoritative among the nations. Even at the foot of Sinai and while Moses was on the mount with God, those perverse Hebrews engaged in rites of blasphemous idolatry. And so it was in their painful history: idolatry, murmuring, rebellion, characterized them. Judgment and mercy characterized God's treatment of them. Many times Moses stood between the guilty people and their offended Monarch, offering to bear in his own person the punishment which they deserved, and interceding for them with prevalent prayer. At the foot of Sinai three thousand men were cut down by the sword for their idolatry. At one time the earth opened and swallowed in its dark vortex a whole company of transgressors. At another time a plague swept away thousands on thousands of the sinning people. Again, fiery serpents whose bite was death invaded their camp, and would have destroyed them altogether had not Moses lifted up among them a brazen serpent upon which if they looked they lived. The forbearance of God toward them is a wonder of history. Moses proved himself to be a patient and brave leader. Slowly the disciplinary pilgrimage wore away. The nations of idolaters were swept from their path. At last, after Miriam and Aaron had died, after a million graves had been dug along the tedious route, and all the adults who came out of Egypt were buried, Moses also died.

He was permitted to behold the promised land, but not to set his foot upon it. From the top of Pisgah he looked upon the Canaan that he loved, to whose border, through incredible hardships, he had led the chosen people. That golden land,—the land of their fathers, the land of their future inheritance, a land flowing with milk and honey, the garden of God,—lay before him. He saw its verdant fields, its silvery streams, its wood-crowned hills, the cities of its pagan people with their works of skill and power. He looked and longed. But his toil and pilgrimage were ended. Alone on that mountain's crest, with his back to the desert, with his face toward Canaan, he died. And God buried him. Human eye hath not seen his grave; human hand hath placed no monument over his sleeping dust. His monument is in his undecaying works. His memorial is the enduring memory of the people of God. The marble has crumbled, the grandest structures of man have perished, but the name and the deeds of Moses are immortal.

The design of the Mosaic commonwealth was of prime importance. The raising up of this indomitable leader, of this wise lawgiver; the succession of stupendous miracles and dreadful judgments which distinguished the early history of Israel; the promulgation of the elaborate code of the Hebrew law; were all tributary to one simple and great design: *the preservation and continuance of the knowledge and worship of Almighty God on earth*. The tendency, as the Scripture narrative shows, as the history and experience of man abundantly attest, is to the forgetfulness of God. Even the fact of the existence of God, that most simple fact, needs to be strongly fortressed that it may not perish from among men. The antediluvians rushed headlong into atheism. At the time of the flood only one man was found true to God; four centuries after the deluge, idolatry and superstition were prevalent; ever since, the world has been alienated from God: heathenism has been the rule. Even now, the majority of the world's population is in pagan night, having no knowledge of the true God. Indeed, it is a startling fact, attested by universal experience and history, that no people has ever retained, or having lost has ever regained, the knowledge of the one eternal Jehovah without some special divine agency in their behalf. God made himself known at first by personal appearance and communication. The call of Abraham, and all the influences of the patriarchal institution, were for the maintenance of the truth respecting God; but the descendants of those patriarchs became idolaters in Egypt, and the most severe agencies which God could employ were hardly sufficient to break them away from their false gods.

Therefore the Hebrew commonwealth was founded, in which God became the national King and the tutelary Deity of that people. He built into the very structure of the Hebrew nationality the knowledge and worship of himself, so that these could not perish while the nation existed. The government was a theocracy. Jehovah was the chief magistrate of the State. The tabernacle was his palace, and there he manifested himself. The prime minister was the high priest. The earthly ruler, whether judge or king, was the viceroy of God. Disobedience was rebellion against God. Religious duty was a political obligation. Prosperity depended upon obedience to the law;

punishment followed its transgression. Religion was not merely the means of vitalizing and strengthening the state, but all the laws and regulations of the state were made the bulwarks of religion. The people were God's people, redeemed by his arm from degrading bondage, rescued by the almighty hand from their enemies. The land of their inheritance was God's land, in which their residence was to be assigned by him and from whose products they were to pay perpetual tithes to him. So God was King, and obedience was maintained by temporal sanctions. Idolatry was treason. The central principle of the theocracy, to which everything else, religious or secular, was subordinate, was the authority and worship of the one only God, Jehovah. For this had wonders been wrought in Egypt. For this the sea was parted. For this the law was proclaimed. For this went forth over the desert the pillar of cloud and fire, the wonder of the nations and the guide of Israel. For this the tabernacle was set up wherein God's glory abode, and the Levites were the palace guards. For this was the succession of miracles, the repetition of judgments and mercies, revealing alike the justice and the compassion of God. For this were established the ordinances and observances which characterized the Hebrew people.

The result has manifested the wisdom of God. Never from the days of Moses have the knowledge and the worship of the one only living and true God been lost on earth. There always has been an Israel, a true people of the Lord, who have loved his character and reverenced his law. And he is to be more widely known and loved: "The earth shall be full of the knowledge of the Lord, as the waters cover the sea."

The world owes much to Moses and to the commonwealth of which he was the founder and head. Raised up in a wonderful manner and fitted for his high commission, that great and good man fulfilled his trust. Never was there another man with whom Jehovah seemed to be so familiar, never another who seemed to have such prevailing influence with God: "There hath not arisen a prophet since in Israel like unto Moses, whom the Lord knew face to face." He loved God and the people of God, " choosing rather to be evil entreated with the people of God, than to enjoy the pleasures of sin for a season; accounting the reproach of Christ greater riches than the treasures of Egypt."

Established in a dark age and one of idolatry, the Hebrew commonwealth attained an influence and power which have to this day controlled a mighty people, while its effects are widely witnessed among the Gentile nations of the globe. It was an economy preparatory to the more perfect one of Christianity, and without which the Christian era could not have been ushered in. The law must precede the gospel. The burning sacrifices offered on the reeking altars of Israel, must precede the great sacrifice offered once for all on Calvary. The system of types and shadows was the herald of the glorious system of redemption.

EPOCH V.

THE PROPHETIC.

THE PROPHETIC.

The prophetic epoch is one wherein great events were transpiring, which also introduces us to a remarkable succession of illustrious men, and during which predictions were uttered that have been slowly fulfilled in the passing of the ages, or are yet to be fulfilled.

There is a charm and an awe which invest the inspired prophets of the Lord. We think of them as a strange, almost supernatural, order, as they have issued forth from their sacred retreat and from communion with God, clad in sackcloth, and boldly declaring in the palaces of kings and before the guilty people the stern and dire messages of Jehovah, the word of the Lord. It is of great interest to study their characters and lives, to mark their influence upon their own and succeeding times, and to observe how, through their agency, God arrested the progress of idolatry and wickedness and national corruption, and maintained religion and the ordinances of true worship.

The prophetic epoch begins with the wise, patriotic, and holy Samuel, the judge and the priest of Israel. There were prophets and prophetic utterances before his time. Abraham and Jacob, and the illustrious Moses, "like unto whom there hath not arisen a prophet since in Israel," had fulfilled some of the functions of the prophetic office. God had promised Moses, "I will raise them up a prophet from among their brethren, like unto thee; and I will put my words in his mouth, and he shall speak unto them all that I shall command him." But with Samuel prophetism assumed the rank and character of an institution. In his day were founded the "schools of the prophets," in which, under the tuition of aged and experienced prophets, young men were trained in sacred literature, to become the moral and religious ministers of the nation. Here they studied the law of Moses, the principles of the theocracy, that they might become their expounders and defenders, and here they attended to the science of sacred music. There were hundreds who were associated and educated in these theological schools, by whose influence, under the control of such instructors as Samuel, Elijah, and Elisha, we may suppose the people of Israel were, to a good degree, brought back from the idolatry and degeneracy which had widely obtained during the administration of the judges. From the time of Samuel, for about seven hundred years, the succession of godly and influential prophets was continued, closing with Malachi, whose last prophetic words of the old era heralded the coming of the prophet-preacher whose solitary voice, sounding in the wilderness, proclaimed the dawn of a more glorious epoch. From Malachi to the Baptist, a period of four hundred years, no prophet's voice was heard.

The prophetic epoch was one of wonderful men and wonderful works. Along its glowing history we may find startling incidents, heroic devotion, unwearied fidelity to God and a faithfulness to men, which paused at no toil nor sacrifice. We behold the chariot of God with its horses of fire descending and bearing away the fearless Elijah, without death, to heaven. We catch the sweet strains of the sweet singer of Israel as he tunes his harp to those songs of Zion which have cheered the Church in days of gloom as well as of triumph. We recognize the boldness and faith of Joel and Hosea and Amos and Micah. We hear the sublime predictions of the evangelical Isaiah as he portrays the Lamb of God, wounded for our sins, led to the slaughter for our justification. We are moved by the mournful lamentations of the weeping Jeremiah, and are roused by the tragic and terrific threatenings of the exiled Ezekiel. We muse with the rapt Daniel as visions of the future pass grandly and gloomily before him, or bow to the lofty tones of the adoring Habakkuk, or rejoice in the cheerful predictions of Haggai and Zechariah. Throughout this entire period there is much to instruct the mind and to stir the heart.

The Hebrew prophets! Let us seek to know who they were, their manner of life and character, their mode of communicating the messages of the Lord and to learn what we may of their history.

The prophets were *inspired men*, who were divinely commissioned to make known the purposes of God and to predict future events. "For no prophecy ever came by the will of man: but men spake from God, being moved by the Holy Ghost." In the earlier days prophets were called seers, indicating their receiving of revelations by visions. They were also called men of God, inspired men, servants and angels of Jehovah, and watchmen. They were holy men, men who loved God and reverenced his law, who were probably chosen for the prophetic office on account of their piety. Sometimes they had been educated by older prophets; sometimes, as in the case of Amos, they were called to their ministry from the common avocations of life. Receiving truth from God by visions or by other modes, they were impelled to declare that truth to those whom it concerned. It is highly probable that the prophetic office was a permanent one; that the call was for life. It was by the agency of the Holy Spirit that the prophets addressed men.

Their *mission* was of great importance. It was designed, not to interfere with any established institutions of the theocracy, but to give vitality and energy to all of them. Provision was early made in the Mosaic law for the prophetic office, and it was under that law, and in it's behalf, that the prophets spoke. This office was entirely distinct from the priesthood. The latter was ordinary, the former was extraordinary. The priests superintended and performed the ritualistic rites and instructed the people in the common duties of religion. But when priests and people became degenerate, when formality had spread through all ranks, or idolatry had assumed the place of true worship, then there was need of an agency which should summon back the recreant priest and the sinful people, which should speak with solemn rebuke and awful warning to both, in the name of the Lord. Such was the mission of the prophets. They were to stand on the downward path and turn back, if possible, the headlong rush of the guilty multitude. They were to reiterate the claims of the holy, but forgotten, law, to declare the jealousy of Jehovah, to proclaim his threatenings and to announce his mercy on condition of repentance and obedience. They were ministers of God; maintaining his authority, guarding the purity and permanency of his sacred ordinances. From their retired communion with God, where in holy visions they received the word of the Lord, they came among men to feel the shock of sin and to be jealous for the Lord of Hosts. Inspired by his Spirit, they became bold in defense of his claims.

They were *preachers of the truth;* proclaiming it when it was forgotten; defending it when it was rejected; explaining it when it was obscure; and ever urging it by the highest motives of interest and of duty. At any sacrifice, at the cost of persecution and imprisonment, even at the risk of life, they were to uphold religion and to denounce idolatry and iniquity.

They were *watchmen:* not only over the people, but over the monarch—over all the interests of the house of Israel. They were the spiritual supervisors and theocratic historians of the nation.

The record of their lives is the testimony of their faithfulness. Alone, relying only upon God, they hurled into the face of kings the charges of their guilt, and pressed home personal responsibility by the declaration, "Thou art the man!" Alone, they arraigned the tumultuous people for their sinful courses and demanded their repentance, lest the vengeance of the Almighty should visit them. It is safe to say that without their agency the chosen people would have become like the heathen nations, and darkness, thick as that which brooded over the antediluvian world, would have hung like a pall around the earth.

It was also a part of their mission *to foretell future events.* Prophecy, in the limited sense, has been a strong bulwark of Christianity. The great fact, standing distinctly forth on the promulgated records of the Scriptures, that events far distant from the time of the prophet who announced them, events which only the divine mind could foreknow, events in historic and still-transpiring series, were plainly foretold and have been as plainly fulfilled—this fact has been and always will be an impregnable argument for our holy religion. The prophets, therefore, acted not alone for their own times and people, but for the universal Church. They furnished an armory of keen weapons for the use of Christian heroes in every age. They demonstrated the divinity of their mission by the prophetic facts which they announced. They gave proof that the Holy Scriptures are indeed the Word of God. The Saviour appealed to what Moses and the prophets had written concerning himself; and out of their own Scriptures demonstrated his Messiahship to the unbelieving Jews. From the sure word of prophecy, as a lamp shining in a dark place, Paul and Peter and the eloquent Apollos drew their convincing arguments. To this source the fathers of the Church in their conflicts with paganism and unbelief confidently resorted. By the proof from prophecy did Justin Martyr and Tertullian and Augustine convince gainsayers. By this has infidelity in every age been put to silence and shame. It furnishes an argument whose force is not diminished by time, but which increases by a constant accumulation of strength as, in age after age, fulfillment follows fulfillment and prophecy is found to be the utterance of the all-knowing God. The mission of the prophets was therefore for the Church and the world to the end of time.

The *character and manner of life* of the prophets may well engage our attention. Their very names represent to us the qualities of goodness and exalted virtue. Moses, Samuel, Elijah, Isaiah, Jeremiah, Ezekiel, Daniel, Habakkuk, Malachi, and the others: holy men, above reproach, worthy messengers and prophets of the Lord! In long and illustrious succession, through hundreds of years, they appeared as the maintainers of religion, loyal among a people inclined to rebellion. Though they were not rich in the wealth of the world, they esteemed themselves the possessors of a priceless inheritance, and the treasures of a nation could not have bought them from the service of God. Though they were not exalted to the high places of the earth, they ranked themselves as above kings and warriors, and they did not hesitate to rebuke iniquity wherever it displayed itself. Though they loved retirement and the lowly walks of a useful life, when the divine call came they pressed out into the din of affairs and had a hand in the stirring transactions of the world. From their acquaintance with God, they learned to esteem rightly the great things of religion, and the little things of the world.

Their life and appearance were humble, and lovers of pleasure may have despised them as they adhered to the simplicity of a holy walk. But no one despised them when from heaven they gave in thrilling tones the messages of Jehovah. Vast assemblages, then, stood awe-struck before them and kings cowered under their denunciations. They were meek men, but their meekness was absorbed by a glowing zeal and an intense devotion when the spirit of inspiration moved them. They were men of real piety. The Spirit who employed them had first sanctified them. They loved God and his law, and they sought to lead the people to the same holy love. For idols and the whole system of idolatry they cherished a withering contempt, which they expressed in graphic and sarcastic language. They had no patience with Hebrew idolaters—with the people of God who voluntarily heathenized themselves: and well they might not have. They would have trampled under their feet every false god, and burnt their polluted altars and slaughtered their impious priests like victims. They did not pause with the ritual and ceremonies of the theocratic code: but as they knew the excellence of true piety they sought to bring others to the experience of it. The malice of men, persecution, death, were things which they did not take into account when duty was before them. To them all men were alike: they saw in the crowned king nothing more of manhood than in the humblest of his menials. Therefore it mattered not to them to whom their message was to be addressed. Samuel did not hesitate to rebuke the sinning Saul. Nathan no more feared to charge his grave crimes upon David than he would have feared to charge them upon Uriah had he been the guilty man. Elijah bearded the idolatrous and tyrannical Ahab wherever he found him. Jeremiah, in the palace and amidst the angry courtiers and armed guards of the king, denounced the wickedness of Zedekiah.

They were strong in the Lord and in the power of his might. Legions of angels guarded their footsteps and the banners of archangels waved around them. On one occasion, when a servant of Elisha feared for his master's safety, the prophet prayed that his eyes might be opened, and "he saw, and behold, the mountain was full of horses and chariots of fire round about Elisha."

Personal success and prosperity were of little moment to them, but the welfare of Israel and Zion's prosperity lay near their hearts. The decay of the chosen people, the desolations which swept as divine scourges over their land, the growth of idolatry and the triumph of the heathen,—these things preyed upon their peace and destroyed their happiness. With a fond and patriotic attachment they loved their country, and there was not one of them who would not gladly have offered himself as a sacrifice in its behalf. They were always jealous for the interests of the nation, and they did not hesitate to rebuke the rash courses and counsels of its kings, to denounce their infamous and treasonable leagues with heathen monarchs, and to summon the people to act as became loyal citizens and true subjects of Jehovah. They were the friends of order, justice and good institutions. They sympathized with the oppressed, the widow and the fatherless. They maintained the rights of humanity, the interests of virtue, the holy ordinances of religion. Though they were bold and severe, the law of kindness dwelt in their hearts, and it was with bitter lamentations that they bewailed the apostasy of the people and the necessity that was upon themselves to rebuke and threaten.

In whatever condition we view the Hebrew prophets, they have the same exalted character, the same excellence and purity of life. Never has there existed a holier order of men, one more worthy the study and imitation of others. Far above the Jewish people, far above the Jewish priests, they tower in the greatness and grandeur of their eminent character, as the few lofty mountain summits loom in solitary majesty above all else, stretching nearer to heaven, and, when darkness rests on things below them, are crowned early and late with the glory of sunlight.

The *modes* in which the prophets communicated the messages of the Lord were various. Sometimes, like orators, they addressed the listening multitudes, in language of calm reasoning or in tones of impassioned eloquence. Thus, Elijah, before the tumultuous thousands of Israel, spoke as one who must impress the intellect and move the feelings of his auditors. "How long halt ye between two opinions? If Jehovah be God, follow him: but if Baal, follow him." Sometimes, in the manner of public heralds, they cried through the streets of the cities, in wild and startling voices, denouncing the coming doom and calling the guilty people to repentance. Thus, in one of the first instances of foreign missionary labor on record, a Hebrew prophet appeared on the streets of a proud and godless heathen city, crying along its populous avenues, as with the thrilling voice of doom, "Yet forty days, and Nineveh shall be overthrown!" Sometimes, they waited to be summoned before nobles and monarchs to give advice, and then seized the opportunity to deliver their message. Thus, after a night of banqueting and revelry in the palaces of Babylon, when the sacred vessels, captured from the Hebrew temple, had been polluted by the impious revelers, and a mysterious hand had come forth and startled the haughty king and his associates by writing their doom upon the wall in letters of fire, Daniel was summoned before Belshazzar, and plainly denounced the crimes of the despot and foretold the overthrow of his power.

At other times they expressed by striking symbols the impending fate of the guilty people, walking before them in sackcloth and with other external marks of anguish. Thus, Jeremiah wore bands and yokes upon his neck, to represent the servitude of some nations. Ezekiel dug through a wall and carried forth his household stuff to symbolize the actions of those who should go into captivity. Again, the prophets recorded the word of the Lord in durable form, to be preserved as a part of the sacred writings of the nation. Hence nearly one-half of the Old Testament consists of their prophetic works, and to the prophets we owe nearly all of the ancient Hebrew Scriptures. It is in their written works that we possess the sweet and magnificent compositions of Isaiah, his sublime predictions of the Messiah; the matchless, mournful elegies of Jeremiah, wherein in plaintive tones he weeps over the desolation of his loved Jerusalem; the tragic and solemn visions of Ezekiel, before whose prophetic foresight passed the ruins of demolished cities and the departed grandeur of proud empires, and on whose enraptured sight rose the Christian commonwealth, the New Jerusalem, the temple of the living God. It is through their treasured writings that we possess the wonderful apocalypse of Daniel, some of which has been fulfilled, some of which awaits fulfillment; together with the prophecies of Joel, Nahum, Habakkuk and their compeers, forming a volume unrivaled in the literature of the world.

The *personal history* of the prophets, at which we can only glance, opens to us incidents that strikingly illustrate their boldness and faith in God and his distinguishing favor to them. In Samuel we see one who, early consecrated to the Lord by a faithful mother, became one of the most illustrious, as he was one of the most godly, of the Hebrew seers, and who, in an age when military prowess was thought to be the first accomplishment in a civil ruler, was raised to the judgeship of Israel through his lofty prophetic character and his intrepidity and success as a religious reformer.

In the life of Elijah we are presented with a rapid succession of heroic deeds and startling miracles, commencing with the abrupt and direful oath before guilty Ahab, "As the Lord, the God of Israel, liveth, before whom I stand, there shall not be dew nor rain these years, but according to my word;" and closing with his sublime translation from earth to heaven by the horses and chariot of fire. Perhaps there is no other one who so thoroughly represents the spirit of the prophetic epoch as this bold and mysterious prophet. Unannounced, with no trace of his pedigree or early life, he appears before the startled Hebrew monarch, with an eye kindled by the fire of inspiration, with a voice ringing like a trumpet-call, clad in the coarse garb of his order, announces his stern message, and passes away. The heavens become like brass over the territories of Israel, and the earth lies scorched and desolate beneath the blaze of an unclouded sun. Famine, disease, death, are the dread results. Three years and a half roll by, and the Hebrew people remains still impenitent. Ahab is their king, Baal is their god. Three years and a half roll by, and the mysterious seer again confronts the impious king. "Is it thou, thou troubler of Israel?" is the quick question of the maddened king. "I have not troubled Israel," was the calm reply of the prophet; "but thou, and thy father's house, in that ye have forsaken the commandments of the Lord, and thou hast followed Baalim." He then demanded that the idolatrous prophets, numbering eight hundred and fifty, should be gathered at Mount Carmel, that the great question, who was the true God, might be signally decided. The mandate of the prophet was obeyed; and from all the towns of Israel, prophets, priests and people thronged on all the thoroughfares which led to the top of Carmel. On the route were the marks of Jehovah's wrath in parched and unproductive fields, in dead bodies of famished animals, in wan and wasted faces and forms of men, women, and children.

An immense multitude swarmed on the summit of the sacred mount at this call of Elijah. Alone and friendless, the holy man stood amidst the great throng, while thousands frowned in hatred upon him. Like a bugle's silvery tone his clear voice rang out on the still air and over the hushed assemblage, "How long halt ye between two opinions? If the Lord be God, follow him: but if Baal, then follow him." Not a word was spoken in reply. He then proposed that two altars should be built, and that a bullock should be laid upon each, and that the God who should answer by fire should be God. All the people answered, "It is well spoken." From morning even until noon, at their cursed altar, the impious priests of Baal invoked the desired result from their god. But there was no answer to their prayers. Excited, they leaped around and upon their altar, while Elijah mocked them and said, "Cry aloud: for he is a god; either he is musing, or he is gone aside, or he is in a journey, or peradventure he sleepeth, and must be awaked." Maddened and frantic, they shouted, and cut themselves with knives and lancets till the blood gushed upon them. But it was all in vain. The day was wearing away, and there was no voice, nor reply, nor any attention to their cries.

It was the hour for the evening sacrifice; Elijah

called the people near him. With twelve stones he rebuilt the altar of the Lord, placed the bullock upon it, and ordered that four barrels of water should be poured upon it once, twice, and the third time. Then, with uncovered head and uplifted hands, he prayed: "O Lord, the God of Abraham, of Isaac, and of Israel, let it be known this day that thou art God in Israel, and that I have done all these things at thy word. Hear me, O Lord, hear me!" Thereupon, fire fell from heaven and consumed the sacrifice and the altar, and all that was upon it or appertained to it, and even the water in the trench around it. With one accord the people fell upon their faces, and they said, "The Lord, he is God! The Lord, he is God!" The prophets of Baal were slain; and on the same day a great rain fell upon the scorched fields of Israel.

The mantle of Elijah fell upon his disciple and friend, Elisha, whose life was signalized by miracles, as had been the life of the former. In deeds of kindness to the widow and the poor, in vindication of the authority of God, in the revival of religion, in the tutelage of prophetic pupils, they spent their days. Others of like spirit succeeded them, who endeavored to perpetuate among their people true spiritual worship of God. They were content to suffer and to sacrifice all worldly things that they might serve God and benefit the nation. In only one do we see high worldly honors associated with devotion and faithfulness to God. At an early age, Daniel was introduced to the royal court of Babylon and educated in the wisdom and learning of the Chaldeans. Although an exile from his native land and exposed to the temptations of a gay and heathen city, he did not yield to the seductions around him, nor did he forget the God of his fathers. True to the religion of Israel, he firmly but courteously refused to comply with the customs of the court, and yet in beauty and knowledge he surpassed his young associates. By the wisdom which God gave him in the interpretation of dreams, he rose, like Joseph in Egypt, to the highest rank in Babylon. Here he was honored with a series of visions and revelations extending through coming ages and embracing some of the most important events in the world's history.

At length the mission of the prophets was ended, and the Hebrew people were blessed no more with their priceless instruction, example, and labors. But the fruits of their work did not perish with their lives. Embodied in the sacred Scriptures, their words have been guarded through the ages; and the men who spake from

God, being moved by the Holy Spirit, still instruct us. The record of their faithfulness and their sacrifices is before us as a worthy and impressive model; to them the apostle points us as examples for our study and imitation.

The more sure word of prophecy remains, as a lamp shining in a dark place, opening a period of greater purity and blessedness than has ever been known on earth, when holiness shall be universal and all the kingdoms of the world shall be the kingdoms of our God. To that epoch the prophets pointed forward; to that day the providences of God are tending. For the coming of that day we should labor and pray.

EPOCH VI.

THE MESSIANIC.

THE MESSIANIC.

Four hundred years of silence, expectation, wonder! Age succeeded age; heaven's counsels seemed to be withdrawn and hidden from the earth. Earth heard no voice of heaven's inspired ambassadors. With the hopeful announcement of the mysterious Malachi, prophecy ceased, and time pressed on to its fulfillment. At length the forerunner, whose coming the last of the prophets had predicted, appeared. Consecrated to his office from his birth, trained for its trying duties amidst the solitudes and divine communion of the wilderness, he was one of the most remarkable of Jehovah's heralds to men. His whole appearance and manner of life attracted the attention of men and gathered the multitudes around him. He was clad in raiment of camel's hair, a leathern girdle was around his loins, and his food was the product of the desert, locusts and wild honey. The pause of centuries was broken by his clarion voice, announcing, "The kingdom of heaven is at hand!" From every quarter of southern Palestine crowds flocked to his wild retreat, to listen to his bold and faithful appeals, and many were baptized of him in Jordan, confessing their sins. The heart of the nation was moved, and in that day of suspense and hope it was not strange that the people questioned whether or not he were the promised Christ. From Jerusalem a delegation of priests and Levites visited him to ascertain the nature of his claims. The Baptist was as humble as he was sincere, and he plainly stated that he was only the harbinger of One mightier than himself, whose shoes' latchet he was not worthy to unloose.

There was a strange baptism at the Jordan. Reluctantly John administered the rite; and at the close of it the vaulted heavens were opened, and the Spirit of God descended gently, like a dove, upon the baptized, and a clear voice spoke from on high, "This is my beloved Son, in whom I am well pleased." The tidings of that extraordinary baptism flew through the land, and men pondered respecting the character and claims of the Messiah.

The Messianic epoch is the great epoch in the world's history. It is the center to which all others converge. Patriarchs and prophets, the saints of the earlier day, looked forward. Apostles and martyrs, the saints of the later day, looked backward. For this period all other periods exist: to it they are subordinate. Around it, as planet around a sun, they all revolve, getting their importance from it and bearing to it their common tribute. The great work of this epoch is that upon which the world depends for its salvation. The life and death of the Redeemer are the confidence and joy of the godly throughout all time. Back at the dawn of human experience, the promise of the Saviour shed some light into the darkened bowers of paradise. The patriarch Abraham rejoiced to see the day of Christ: and he saw it, and was glad. The reign of the Messiah awoke the sublimest strains of the sweet psalmist of Israel. The prophets foretold the coming and work of Immanuel. In the Redeemer who was to come, the pious, through the preparatory centuries, hopefully trusted. The sacrifices smoking on a thousand altars, the bloody rites administered by consecrated priests, were types of the great Sacrifice once for all offered for the sin of the world.

Since his death, the pious have trusted in the Saviour who has come. Apostles pointed to Calvary, and they taught that the blood there shed was all-sufficient. The cross became the impressive symbol of the Christian faith. With the name of Christ upon their lips, though in the arena and amidst the flames, martyrs have died in triumph. With faith in him, saints in all the ages have found peace in life, and victory in death.

As the Messianic epoch was the terminating point of all that went before it, so was it the starting point of all that came after it. Like the Spirit, the central guiding power amidst the uplifted and revolving wheels and living creatures in the vision of Ezekiel, so is the Messiah, amidst the revolving wheels of providence and the living energies which sway the nations and the changing dispensations of the ages, the center and the soul of all. If we cannot fully grasp the spirit of that era and enter into the life which animated it and comprehend the work that was fulfilled then, we can perhaps attain to some approximation to what we would desire.

The *advent* of the Prince of Peace took place at a pacific period of the world's history.

> "No war, or battle's sound,
>   Was heard the world around:
>   The idle spear and shield were high uphung:
>   The hooked chariot stood
>   Unstained with hostile blood,
>   The trumpet spoke not to the armed throng;
>   And kings sat still, with awful eye,
>   As if they surely knew their sov'reign Lord was by."

The conquering legions of Rome had borne her invincible eagles from land to land, and from Gaul to India the nations reposed beneath its sheltering sway. A kind of hush was upon the world, broken only by a low tone, like that which is said to precede a great convulsion in nature,

> "When from the shores
> And forest-rustling mountains comes a voice
> That, solemn-sounding, bids the world prepare!"

Never had there been a time so opportune for the mission of the Christ. The fullness of the time had come for that event which prophecy had announced and for which Providence had been for ages perfecting its designs. The world was open for the spread of Christianity. Along the great thoroughfares that Rome had built to her remotest provinces, on which her couriers flew and over which her legions could be poured, the heralds of the cross could safely journey. The arts and arms of the conquerors had done much toward banishing the ignorance and improving the manners of barbarian states. No exciting subject occupied the attention and energies of the nations. They were in a waiting posture.

Especially were the Hebrews looking and longing for their Deliverer, whose coming the patriarchs had foreseen and the prophets foretold. Some, like the good old Simeon and the pious Anna, entertained correct views of the spirituality of his mission. But the great majority cherished false sentiments to which their pride and selfishness prompted. Their restless spirits fretted under the foreign yoke and they hoped for rescue when their Messiah should appear. Misinterpreting the prophesies of their sacred books, they came to regard him as a temporal prince, whose prowess should restore the ancient supremacy of the Hebrew commonwealth. Divided into sects clashing among themselves, crushed under the imperious tread of their conquerors, and dead to the spirit of their ancient faith and worship, the Jews were in a pitiable state; they were not prepared for the reception of a saviour such as Jesus. "He came unto his own, and they that were his own received him not."

The circumstances of his advent were peculiar. There was a mingled lowliness and greatness which characterized the Messiah from the first—the humbleness of humanity with the exaltation of divinity. He was the Son of God; yet he was born of a virgin. An angel voice, in the stillness of night, announced his birth to shepherds who were watching their flocks, and angel choirs celebrated the event in sublimest anthems. Yet on that night the newborn Christ was cradled in a manger. To the obscure home of his parents came Magi from the East, presenting costly offerings and paying reverence to him as to an infant prince. Like other children, he was carried to the temple to be presented to the Lord, but there the inspired Simeon and the prophetess Anna welcomed him as the Hope of Israel. In his coming there was no outward pomp, no regal nor military splendor; all was humility, the hidings of divinity. For a time the wonders that marked his advent may have impressed the people, but in the retirement of Nazareth Jesus was forgotten; the memory of those wonders was preserved by few. His presence, when a lad, among the doctors of the temple, where he manifested a wisdom far surpassing his years, may have revived, to a limited extent, the earlier impressions; but again he passed away into a deeper obscurity than before.

Galled and crushed under the Roman power, with no harmony among themselves, and having but little that was bright in the future, their temple pillaged and its worship declining, the Hebrew people were in a mournful condition. The proud Pharisees looked with scorn upon all others and dwelt apart in their hypocritical sanctity. The Sadducees, self-confiding and bent on ease and pleasure, denied the greatest truths of man's being and cared for little else than their own temporal gratification. The Essenes, indulging in sickly revery and aiming at a sort of transcendental experience, severed their connection with society and frittered away the facts of religion. The multitude, more debased than their superiors, imitated only the vices of those above them and plunged more deeply into sin. Accordingly, the state of the Jews at large was mournful indeed. Ignorance, profligacy, wickedness, abounded, and little of their ancient character and customs was left save a blind devotion to the externals of the Mosaic institutions. Their traits appear repulsive; their acts are those of obdurate and cruel men.

Among such people, at this era, a divine Life was introduced. The Word became flesh and dwelt among men, full of grace and truth. By the mysterious union of the divine and human natures, Jesus was prepared for his redemptive and mediatorial work.

It is difficult to grasp or to describe *the life of the Saviour*. It was unique and excellent: Godlike, and therefore beyond comparison with all others; human, and therefore resembling the life of all men. The life of Jesus transcends all other lives: from the most perfect of men we look with adoring contemplation to Christ, as from the best human works we turn to the handiwork of the great

Creator. From every point of view we are impressed with the same pre-eminence of his life. As a child, as a friend, as a teacher, as an example, as Redeemer, Jesus stands alone. From the morning of his days until the evening, he is wonderful, God manifest in the flesh.

Of his childhood we know but little. Then he was the delight of the family, a solace and a wonder to his mother, who in her heart pondered his sayings and actions. Of his manhood the records are sufficient to show that in him every grace and excellence met. He was meek and lowly, with no aspirations for earthly distinction; and to the tempter he presented no vulnerable point. His kingdom was not of this world. When he was reviled, he reviled not again; when he suffered he threatened not. He was gentle among the arrogant; forgiving and kind to those who wronged him. Like a lamb he was led even to the slaughter. In him we see a condescension that never can be paralleled. It is seen not only in his coming into the world, but also in the manner in which he came, and in all his life after he came. He was God's own Son, yet he became the Son of man. He was accustomed to the dignities of heaven, yet he took a low place among the people of the world. Turning away from the powerful and learned in their places of pride, he sought the society of the humble and needy. His parents were in lowly life: to them he became obedient. From those who were engaged in the common occupations of life he summoned twelve to be his apostles. To the poor he preached the gospel. On foot, often alone, he went about doing good, sought more by those who looked to him for benefits than by those who desired to benefit him. Though the treasures of the universe were at his disposal, he was often in want; though the Creator of all worlds, he had not where to lay his head. Though he was rich, yet for our sakes he became poor. Though he might have had holy society, he mingled with those who had no love for his character, no regard for his claims. For others' welfare he sacrificed ease, time, comfort, bodily rest, the things that men are accustomed to prize. He pleased not himself.

He called his disciples, friends. As an example to them, he washed their feet. He ate with publicans and sinners. He came to seek and to save the lost.

Children were his delight. His gentle nature found gratification in their innocent manners and loving disposition; he welcomed their presence, and they rejoiced in him. He taught his disciples to become as little children. He was a man of sorrows, and acquainted with grief. He humbled himself not merely to a lowly life, but he became obedient unto death, even the death of the cross.

His self-denial was unequaled. Instead of the joy that was set before him, he consented to undergo the shame and pain of his earthly life.

His compassion was godlike. With deep concern, with intense sympathy, he beheld the miserable condition of men. Over Jerusalem he wept as with the grief of a father. Among the sinful and the suffering he walked with a heart whose compassion embraced all their woes, which went down to the lowest and vilest and sought the welfare of all. His pity led to the exercise of his divine attributes. To him the people were like sheep without a shepherd, and he longed to be their Shepherd. The claims of the poor, the wants of the widow and fatherless, the afflictions of the wretched in body or in mind, appealed to his heart, and he was swift to afford them sympathy and aid.

It were difficult to enumerate all the excellences of his character as they were illustrated in his wonderful life. He was bold, patient, discreet. In wisdom he surpassed the sages of the world. A greater than Solomon was he.

His forgiveness was divine. For his worst enemies he prayed earnestly. In purity and temperance, in love to God and benevolence to men, he far outranked all that the world has elsewhere witnessed. He loved the world, and the untiring devotion of his whole life was a testimony to the depth and strength of that love. No labor was too arduous, no danger to imminent, no sacrifice too painful, no time too precious, for securing the salvation of sinners. From place to place he journeyed till his way-worn frame was almost exhausted. Then, famishing, and resting on the well's cold curb, he sought to lead the sinning to God. Depriving himself of needful sleep, he spent whole nights in prayer in the solitudes of the mountains.

His benevolence did not exhaust itself in a life of activity, toil, and sacrifice. It led him to sufferings such as no one else has ever endured, to a death whose strange and painful character awoke even the sympathy of inanimate nature. Such was Jesus. For us he travailed, wept, died.

These separate excellences of character and life were harmoniously combined in Christ, while at the same time they were unmingled with the frailties and imperfections of humanity, thus forming a model, beautiful, proportionate, consistent, divine. It was God with us.

The *works* of Christ were more striking to the people of his day than was his life. The latter was, naturally, to a great degree retired and unknown by the world. Much of his time was spent with his chosen disciples, much was spent in places aloof from the busy and turbulent crowd. But the former were public and palpable, and fitted to produce a deep impression on all who witnessed them. They were the tokens of divinity. They commenced with the ministry of Christ and they continued to its close. They open to us a succession of facts, not indeed as stupendous as those which characterized the Mosaic economy, but more in harmony with the spirit of Christianity and the claims of its Founder. They were works of kindness and benevolence, fitted to promote human happiness and to diminish human suffering. Seldom for himself, often for others, did he employ his divine attributes in miraculous works. The condition of the blind, the deaf, the dumb, touched the sympathetic heart of Jesus. All the suffering excited his commiseration and he delighted to help and relieve them.

In his day men suffered with a peculiar and awful infliction known as demoniacal possession. The effects of this possession were dreadful. Men were torn and lashed to fury; they were deprived of the use of their physical and mental faculties by the demon within them. Life was made a misery to themselves and a terror to others. Christ mercifully released many from the presence and terrific tyranny of evil spirits. They recognized his authority and stood in awe of him. *Men* might doubt as to his claims, but *these* cried out, " We know who thou art, thou Holy One of God!"

The cause and effects and history of this dreadful malady and scourge are imperfectly understood and perhaps cannot be explained. It may be that as Satan and his minions knew of the mission of Christ and his advent, they were moved to oppose him, to do what they could to check his influence, to thwart his designs, and so at about the time of his birth made an irruption from hell, adopted a new mode of assault, by this series of diabolical movements. As Christ was to become miraculously united to human nature, so they possessed men and tried to counteract his work.

The manner in which Jesus rebuked and defeated them, probably put a speedy end to their new and fiendish plans. At Gadara there were two men possessed with devils, who had their haunts among the tombs. They are described as exceeding fierce, night and day wandering in the mountain and amongst the sepulchers of the dead, attacking those who passed near them, crying with loud voices, cutting their naked bodies with sharp stones, and, whenever bound, snapping asunder their chains and fetters and escaping.

By the word of Jesus the evil spirits were expelled, and the poor men sat at the feet of their deliverer, clothed and in their right mind. We are told of a youth who was seized by an evil spirit, and torn so that he uttered cries of woe and foamed and gnashed his teeth and pined away, and sometimes fell into fire and again into water. Jesus, at the request of the youth's father, rebuked the foul invader, and banished him from his usurped dominion. But his departure was attended with such anguish that for a time the child seemed to be dead.

In multitudes of similar cases, Christ illustrated his power and benevolence. He was ever ready to relieve human sorrow and suffering, and no one who applied to him was repulsed or sent away unblessed. His ear was ever open to the cry of the desolate-hearted; to the humblest he bent with manifest sympathy; for the sinful and wretched he was prompt to exercise his divine attributes. His own wants were forgotten in behalf of those whom he came to benefit and to save. He healed the sick; he recalled the dead to life: wherever he went fountains of gladness and blessing gushed forth. A kind of heavenly atmosphere surrounded him, and whoever came within its influence was healed and sanctified.

Touching instances of his compassionate works are given by the evangelists. A popular poet of our own has gracefully rendered one of them:

> Blind Bartimeus at the gates
> Of Jericho in darkness waits;
> He hears the crowd;—he hears a breath
> Say, It is Christ of Nazareth!
> And calls in tones of agony,
> Ιησοῦ, ἐλέησόν με!
>
> The thronging multitude increase:
> Blind Bartimeus, hold thy peace!
> But still, above the noisy crowd,
> The beggar's cry is shrill and loud;
> Until they say, He calleth thee!
> Θάρσει, ἐγείραι, φωνεῖ σε!
>
> Then saith the Christ, as silent stands
> The crowd, What wilt thou at my hands?
> And he replies, Oh give me light!
> Rabbi, restore the blind man's sight!
> And Jesus answers, Ὕπαγε,
> Ἡ πίστις σου σέσωκέ σε!
>
> Ye that have eyes, yet cannot see,
> In darkness and in misery,
> Recall those mighty voices three,
> Ιησοῦ, ἐλέησόν με!
> Θάρσει, ἐγείραι, ὕπαγε!
> Ἡ πίστις σου σέσωκέ σε!

Amongst all his works of wonder, none more fully illustrated his great benevolence than the three instances which are given of his restoring the dead to life. In these three cases there is a remarkable gradation as respects the period during which the persons had been dead.

At the south of Mount Tabor was the city of Nain. In his walk through Galilee, the Saviour approached that city, attended by his chosen disciples and a concourse of people. He had delivered his matchless Sermon on the Mount, that had astonished the people by the truthfulness and authority of its doctrine, which far surpassed the teachings of the scribes. On the previous day he had restored from sickness the servant of a pious Roman centurion, whom, though at a distance and unseen, he cured by his word. Now the crowd, undoubtedly, expected further wonders. As the Messiah, his disciples, and the reverential people came near the walls of Nain, they met a funeral procession issuing from the gate. It was the funeral of a young man, the only son of his mother, who was a widow. Many of the people of the city expressed their sympathy for the bereaved mother, accompanying her to the burial of her son. As Jesus beheld the weeping woman in her loneliness and anguish, his sympathy was stirred. Perhaps he thought of his own mother whom he tenderly loved. Approaching the mourner, he said in compassionate tones, "Weep not!" He touched the bier, and the procession stopped. It was a moment of suspense to the friends and to the multitude. The voice of Jesus broke the stillness, saying, "Young man, I say unto thee, Arise!" The pale form arose, the tides of life flowed again in their wonted channels, and he began to speak. To the amazed and silent mother the Redeemer delivered her lost son. Fear fell upon every beholder, and as they passed solemnly away, one said, "A great prophet is arisen among us," and another, "God hath visited his people."

Capernaum was a chief seat of the Saviour's teachings and miracles. Once, a ruler of the synagogue there came and fell before him, beseeching him to come and heal his daughter, a child of twelve years, who was at the point of death. Jesus at once went with the father, who was anxious lest his daughter should die before they could reach the house. On the road word was brought to the ruler that the child was dead. Jesus comforted him with the promise that she should yet live. Arriving at the house, Jesus, with only the parents and three of his favored disciples, entered the chamber where the dead lay. Quickly, without ostentation, he took the hand of the maiden, simply saying, "Maiden, arise." Her spirit returned and she rose up immediately, to the amazement of her parents.

In the little village of Bethany, near Jerusalem, lived a family to whom Jesus was tenderly attached, Martha, Mary and their brother Lazarus. The brother was taken sick, and the sisters sent to Christ the affectionate message, "Lord, behold, he whom thou lovest is sick." Before the tidings reached the Master, Lazarus had died; and when Jesus came to the house it was to hear from the bereaved sisters the lament, "Lord, if thou hadst been here our brother had not died." Jesus wept. He loved Martha and her sister and Lazarus. Their sorrow was his sorrow. With them, Martha calm and resigned, Mary bowed in excess of grief, and with his disciples, Jesus came to the grave. It was a cave, and a stone lay against it. Jesus directed them to remove the stone, which they did. He then led the little company in prayer. The prayer was ended, and for a moment all was still by the silent grave. Then he cried with a loud voice, "Lazarus, come forth!" He that was dead came forth, bound hand and foot with grave-clothes: and his face was bound about with a napkin.

The miraculous works of Jesus were frequent and impressive; yet they had but little effect upon the mass of the people. Many, indeed, believed on him, but the great majority felt indifferent to his claim while they were reproved by his life. Those who had authority and influence, as a general thing, became his enemies and even plotted for his death.

The *teachings* of Jesus were in harmony with his works and his life. They were of a lofty character and fell on the ears of men as with the voice of divinity. There was a tone terrible and withering in his rebukes. Pharisees and scribes, sinners of every grade, cowered in his majestic presence when he denounced woes upon them for their crimes. When he spoke before assemblies of the people, they listened as to no common teacher. We read, "The multitudes were astonished at his teaching: for he taught them as one having authority, and not as their scribes." The mingled simplicity and wisdom of his words fell upon them like tones from heaven, and charmed while they instructed and reproved. There was in his simplest speech a power which they could not withstand. On one occasion his enemies sent officers to take him; so awed were they by his language and bearing that they returned without him, and gave as their excuse to those who had sent them, "Never man so spake." On another occasion an armed band, with murderous intent, invaded his retirement to capture him. Jesus came forth to them and asked whom they sought, and when they told him, "Jesus of Nazareth," he said, "I am he:" whereupon those rude men went backward and fell to the ground.

He went down to the place where he had spent his childhood and preached in their synagogue on the Sabbath. The people who heard him were astonished and wondered at the words of grace which proceeded out of his mouth. At the great assemblies on the occasions of the annual feasts of the nation he spoke as with the authority of God. He presented the claims of his kingdom as supreme, and demanded the loyalty of the human heart for himself. He set forth a spiritual dispensation which, in the passing away of the old dispensation, should run parallel with the life of the race and should have the allegiance of the world. He lifted men's minds to a higher standpoint than they had before attained, and gave to the people a broader range of vision than the old economy had contemplated. He exalted the divine law and gave its sanctions a new impressiveness and a stronger grasp on the life of man. At the same time he revealed the way of reconciliation to which the earliest prophecies had pointed and which had been typified in the sacrifices of the Levitical code.

He taught of God, and set up in his Church, as one of its perpetual sacraments, an enduring monument to the mysterious Trinity of the Godhead. Of the final judgment and the future state he spoke truth that was of overshadowing and supreme importance and that was fitted to move all the sensibility of the soul. With all that there was of dignity, force, and awfulness in his teaching, there was also a tenderness and love which marked him as a sympathizing Saviour. He had words of solace for the smitten hearts of mourners, words of pity for the miserable and convicted sinners, words of kindly warning for the reckless wanderers from God. To the wretched and despairing he said, "Come unto me, all ye that labor and are heavy-laden, and I will give you rest." Over those about to perish, he wept with bitter lamentation. To the saddened disciples whom he was soon to leave, he spoke words of affection and cheer. His instructions were adapted to men as they are, and to their peculiar needs. Christ was a practical teacher. He taught men how to live, how to be ready for the future life. He required holiness of men—a holiness which, being supreme in the soul, should control the conduct and lead to resemblance to God. The ancient economy was "the bond written in ordinances," and although God designed that it should foster a spiritual religion, yet the Jews had made it void by their traditions. Christ reasserted the claims of the moral law, enthroned it in supreme authority, and swept away the cumbersome ceremonies of an earlier dispensation. He taught that God takes cognizance of the hidden motives and designs, and judges not so much from the external manifestation as from the internal principle. And this is a cardinal, distinctive feature of the Master's instruction.

Notwithstanding the godlike life, the miraculous works, and the heavenly instructions of Jesus, he was not acknowledged and received by the world. In accordance with ancient prophecy, he was despised and rejected of men. All along in his divine ministry there had been those who desired and plotted his destruction. His goodness was his greatest crime. They who felt rebuked by his holy life and teachings, feared his influence and hated his power. In his triumph they foresaw their own downfall. Rulers, scribes, priests, saw that their authority was waning before the power of his influence and that the people were yielding to his claim. They said, " The world is gone after him." Here and there, also, one and another among the learned and influential were convinced that he was the true and promised Messiah. His enemies took counsel how they might take Jesus and kill him.

For the last time the toil-worn Teacher came

up from his wanderings to the sacred Hebrew capital. He came in triumph. From Olivet multitudes thronged his pathway and escorted him with regal honors. They spread their garments and branches of trees in his path. With loud exultations they cried, "Hosanna! Blessed is he that cometh in the name of the Lord!" From the city other multitudes came out to meet him and give him welcome. Not since the days of Israel's kings had such a triumph been witnessed in the city of David. The whole city was moved. He came to the temple and there healed the blind and the lame, while the children hailed him with their hosannas. During that passover week he continued his instructions and warnings to the people. More insidiously than ever his enemies conspired for his death. They found a traitor in one of his own apostles. The plot thickened around the person of Christ.

Unmoved by all that was transpiring, Jesus, with his disciples, partook of the solemn feast of the nation. The city was crowded with those who had come from all parts of Palestine and from foreign marts of trade, to participate in the gorgeous and scenic ceremonies of that festival week. To none was it more full of thrilling interest than to the little group, Jesus and his apostles, in an upper chamber of the capital. Years before, after the manner of the old philosophers, he had called them from their humble occupations to accompany him in his labors and to learn from him of the realities of his kingdom. The philosophy which he taught them was superior to any which the schools had taught. Although of widely dissimilar traits, their personality had been greatly modified by their intimate intercourse with One so exalted and heavenly. The impetuous Peter and the loving John were there, the two most interesting members of the group. There was the sincere and guileless Bartholomew, and James, the first apostolic martyr. Around that table were men who were to leave strong impressions on the thought of the world and were to introduce the grandest revolution in human history, written not in blood and sorrow, on ensanguined plains, with slaughtered thousands, but in penitences and prayers and lives of holiness and blessed service in the eternal heavens.

As they partook of the paschal supper, Jesus instituted a new sacrament, to be observed when the Hebrew passover should be forgotten, in perpetual memorial of his atoning work for the world, the new Supper of the Lord, commemorating by simple symbols his body which was broken and his blood which was shed for the sins of mankind. The minds of the apostles were unprepared for such an occasion, and it was with bewildering doubt and fear that they passed through the solemnities of that remarkable evening. Mournful to them must have been the voice of their Master, as with them he chanted, "The cords of death compassed me: I found trouble and sorrow," or as in exulting strains they sang, "The stone which the builders rejected is become the head of the corner." Most affecting must have been those petitions which he offered in the fullness of his affection and solicitude for them. It was a night long to be remembered by the apostles of our Lord.

The hush of midnight was on the homes of Jerusalem when Jesus and his disciples passed along its deserted streets, across the flowing Kedron to the garden of Gethsemane, where he was accustomed to go for retirement and prayer. For the last time he entered this lonely retreat where he had often found strength for duty and trial in communion with his Father. A deep shadow passed over the soul of Jesus at that midnight hour. It was midnight in his heart. Sorrow poured, like surging waves, through his soul. He said, "My soul is exceeding sorrowful, even unto death." He earnestly asked his three beloved disciples to watch with him. Alone he passed into the deeper shadows of the garden, and prayed that, if it were possible, he might be spared the sufferings that were appointed for him. "Nevertheless," he said, "not as I will, but as thou wilt." An angel came from heaven to strengthen him in that supreme trial. But his agony increased, and his only help was in prayer. Again and again he sought support where only the wounded and suffering can ever find the help which they must have. God gave him strength for the approaching ordeal, and calmly he announced that the time for his betrayal had come.

Hardly had he spoken when the glare of approaching torches flickered through the groves of olive trees and the tread of armed men rang along the paths leading to Gethsemane. Judas, the traitor, was at their head, leading them to the hallowed spot consecrated by the agony and prayer of the Son of God. Those rude men laid hands on Jesus and hurried him to the house of the high-priest. Dismayed and perplexed, the apostles deserted him and fled, leaving him alone with his enemies.

The story of his *trial* is brief and saddening. He was brought before the Sanhedrin, whose members hated him and had long desired his death. False witnesses testified against him. The high-priest perverted his language to blasphemy. With one voice, they all condemned him to death.

Perished was the ancient Hebrew justice! Perished was the grandeur of the old Mosaic law, which for thousands of years had been the bulwark of human freedom and of personal rights! Perished was the sacred character of the chief priest of the venerated Hebrew religion! By the highest Jewish tribunal, the Son of God, the Messiah of that favored nation, the Saviour of the world, was pronounced worthy of death! Darkest picture, saddest scene in the jurisprudence of the world!

But they could not enforce their condemnation. Roman law was supreme in the Hebrew metropolis, and that stern and potent law guarded the life of every individual wherever the eagles of the empire testified to its sway. Behold the priests and elders of the Jews, and the scribes, hurrying in the early morning to the palace of Herod, where Pilate, the Roman procurator, was then residing! Witness their eagerness to prejudice and overawe the Roman judge; their thirst for the blood of Jesus! At first they touched the jealous nature of Pilate, then they appealed to his fears, and at last, when the weak magistrate had yielded step by step before them, when he had scourged the innocent Redeemer and had brought him forth, wounded and bleeding, to their presence, as if the sight of blood only maddened them the more, they cried out, with tumultuous voices, "Crucify him! Crucify him!" Their ferocious mandate was obeyed, and Roman justice fell prostrate before Jewish malice and frenzy.

After this followed a succession of scenes of the most painful nature. Jesus was given up to the rudeness and insolence of the rough soldiery. They clothed him in purple and crowned him with thorns and gave him a reed for a scepter, and with mock reverence kneeled before him as before an earthly king. Insult followed indignity. They spit upon him and smote him and knelt at his feet in derisive worship.

Amidst these abhorrent scenes a terrible tragedy was enacted. The traitor Judas, stung with remorse, hurled at the feet of those who had hired him the price of blood, and rushed from the temple and hanged himself. For him Mercy could not plead, and Justice could not tarry. He went to his own place, a fearful witness to the fact of human depravity and a dreadful instance of the certainty of divine retribution.

It was nearly nine o'clock in the morning, when a strange procession passed forth from Jerusalem on the way to Calvary. First went the mail-clad soldiery of Rome; then the meek Redeemer, almost exhausted by the endurance of the morning and the agony of the preceding night; next, a black man bearing the cross, and then a great company of the friends of Jesus, bewailing his fate with loud lamentations. On Golgotha was the *Crucifixion.*

Christ died for man. The burden of a world's transgression was laid upon him. In that death he finished the work that was given him to do.

Nature expressed her sympathy for her suffering Creator. For three long hours darkness was spread like a pall over all the land. As by unseen hands the veil of the temple was torn in twain. An earthquake shook the city and rent the ancient hills. Graves were opened and the sheeted dead walked forth, went into the holy city, startling those to whom they appeared. Fear fell upon the centurion and his soldiers, and they exclaimed, "Truly this was the Son of God!"

On the third day of his sepulture, an angel stood at the tomb, and at his presence the earth quaked and the keepers became as dead men. Victorious over death, *Christ arose!*

For a little season the Redeemer appeared to his wondering disciples and blessed them with his presence, his counsels, and prayers. On a mountain of Galilee, he communed with above five hundred of his assembled disciples. Finally from Jerusalem he led his apostles out near to Bethany, where he blessed them. Then he was parted from them, and, environed in a cloud, he rose to heaven, where he ever liveth to make intercession for his friends.

So ends the wondrous Messianic epoch, the central epoch of the world's history. We pass back over the life of the adorable Saviour, recalling his lowly parentage, his eminent and holy character, his benevolent and miraculous works; we listen to his godlike teachings and learn of his superhuman sufferings, and we know that all this was for us. For us Christ is the Way, the Truth, the Life. He is our Brother, our Friend, our Teacher, our Redeemer, our Lord.

EPOCH VII.

THE APOSTOLIC.

THE APOSTOLIC.

GALILEE was the northern of the three great divisions of Palestine; Samaria was the southern; Judea lay between them. Galilee was itself divided into two portions, upper and lower. The upper portion, at the time of Christ, was inhabited by various clans, fragments of surrounding nations, who had found secure retreats among the fastnesses of its protecting mountains. The lower portion was the residence of a brave, high-spirited, industrious, and independent people, who spurned the Roman yoke and were ever ready for sedition. Here Jesus lived, here he taught and wrought his miracles, here he selected his apostles, and here he showed himself to his disciples after his resurrection.

Some of the towns of Galilee were Bethsaida, Cana, Capernaum, Chorazin, Nain, Nazareth, Tiberias—names which recall interesting scenes in the life and history of Jesus and his apostles.

The character and occupations of the people were more favorable for the work of Jesus than were those of the people of Judea. The influence of the metropolis, with its pride and bigotry, its clashing sects and degenerate morals, had not extended into Galilee. And although there were rudeness and ignorance which, at first, might be thought to detract from the capability of the Galilean people, yet these were associated with other traits, which, sanctified and guided, would produce the qualifications and character that Jesus sought in the men, who, at that epoch, in the face of opposition and at the risk of life, were to propagate the new religion of which he was the Founder.

Jesus and his apostles were Galileans. In that obscure region, from humble beginnings, Christianity entered upon its career of conquest. At first, as we have seen, a single Person appeared, ushered before men by divine tokens and revealing attributes of deity. Slowly his kingdom made its way against the prejudice and hostility of Judaism; then, emerging from its Galilean home, it took position within the sacred precincts of the temple, and demanded the confidence and loyalty of the ancient people of God; and then in its resistless progress it went onward over the trembling shrines and temples of paganism, until Christianity wore upon its own brow the diadem of the Cæsars and swayed its scepter over the known world. Although from age to age its successes and reverses have alternated, yet now it is widely extending its triumphs and faithfully working for universal dominion.

To the teachings and example of the apostles may be traced the zeal and self-denial and world-wide benevolence which, in every period following theirs, have characterized their successors. As we pass back to the review of their lives and times we find the noblest exemplifications of the faith and heroism which the gospel is fitted to nurture; we see the spirit of Christianity developed in lives of supreme devotion, pausing at no personal sacrifice or danger, and leading on through persecution to the martyr's death and the martyr's crown; nor can we fail to find the wonderful results which followed such faith and devotion.

Soon after Jesus had entered on his public ministry, he sought for a select number of disciples, to be with him as personal friends and companions, to whom he could impart the great things of his kingdom and who would remain as witnesses of his godlike life and instructions after he should have gone away. He selected men whom he deemed to be fitted for the station and work of the apostleship. He did not seek them among the wealthy and influential families of Judea, whose position and power might have been considered desirable as an aid to his cause. He did not go to the Hebrew schools and choose those who had been thoroughly educated in the law and theology of the nation, and whose learning and eloquence might have been thought most important for gaining adherents to the gospel. He went to the uneducated, courageous, and independent Galileans; he chose men who were unknown to the world, who were free from the prejudices and pride which prevailed through all ranks of the learned and powerful; men who were bound to no sect, who had nothing of station or reputation to lose by becoming the followers of the Nazarene, and who under the tuition of Jesus would become zealous and faithful apostles.

He called four fishermen from the Sea of Galilee, telling them that he would make them "fishers of men." He called a collector of customs from his business, and others from common pursuits of life, simply saying to them, "Follow me." They left all and followed him. With a self-denial, devotion, and affection which are marvelous, they attached themselves to the mysterious Teacher whose instruction and works were then attracting the attention of men in every department and business of life. Throughout his ministry they were his constant companions, his attentive disciples. Although at first they could not appreciate his instructions, and although it was hard for them to understand the spirituality of his kingdom, yet Jesus knew that through his continued teachings and training they would eventually be enlightened to grasp what he should reveal to them. They held the Jewish belief respecting the Messiah, which was that he would come as a temporal prince to free the nation from the yoke of its oppressors and to restore its ancient power and glory. Accordingly they were constantly looking forward to the time when their Master should throw off his disguise, summon the enthusiastic people to his banner, and lead them forth to victory. No doubt they were ready for the conflict which they anticipated. The miraculous power of Jesus gave them confidence in him as a leader. The commissariat was dependent only on his word. They saw five thousand men abundantly fed with five loaves and two fishes, and they knew of no limit to his ability. They saw him walking upon the sea as upon dry land. They saw him restoring the dead to life, giving soundness and strength to the lame, the sick, and to those afflicted with any malady. What could not such a chieftain accomplish? He could feed his armies in a desert; he could bring back to life those who should fall in battle, and restore the wounded by his word. No defeat, no reverses, would be felt by one who possessed such recuperative forces.

It was hard for the apostles to learn that the kingdom of their Lord was a spiritual kingdom. They discussed the matter of their relative rank when he should sit upon his throne. Even after his resurrection, after all that they had heard from Jesus before his betrayal, and had seen in the experiences of his death, they asked him, " Lord, dost thou at this time restore again the kingdom to Israel?" So difficult was it for them to renounce their long-cherished views. Their training, therefore, was directed to that point. Christ inculcated upon them those virtues which would distinguish them from the world—humility, self-denial, forgiveness of injuries, devotion to God. By his own impressive example he taught them what their lives should be. They saw in him a perfect model. While he had no conformity to the world, he had the deepest sympathy and benevolence for the world. He was untiring in labor, constant in prayer, watchful for opportunity to say and to do the best thing for others. To his apostles he freely spoke. He made known to them, so far as they could bear it, the truth respecting himself, respecting their mission, respecting God and his government. So they were under a discipline eminently fitted to prepare them for their responsible and laborious life. From him they heard instruction which was adapted to their condition. In him they saw the exemplification of what their own lives should be.

The *apostolic office* was peculiar. Strictly speaking the apostles had no successors. They were succeeded by those who entered into their labors, who partook of their spirit, who were instructed and ordained by them for the work of preaching the gospel. Those who have most of their faith and devotion in this work and in love to Christ, are most like the apostles. But as apostles they stood alone. The qualifications for the office did not exist after their day. It was necessary that they should have *seen the Lord*, and should have personally witnessed what they declared to men. The apostles recognized this necessity in their choice of Matthias. Paul also bases the proof of his apostleship on this ground. He says, "Am I not an apostle? have I not seen Jesus our Lord?" plainly implying that the seeing of Christ was essential to his being an apostle. Elsewhere he declares, "Last of all, as to a child untimely born, he appeared to me also." It was necessary that an apostle should be immediately called and chosen to the apostolic office by Christ himself.

Infallible inspiration was also a necessary qualification for the office. Without this they could not have discharged their mission. It belonged to them not only to unfold the meaning of the ancient sacred writings of the Hebrews, but also to embody in their own new Scriptures the principles and constitution of the Christian commonwealth. They were to give the world a new revelation, the authoritative and permanent guide of the Church of Christ to the end of time. They needed therefore what was promised to them and what was bestowed upon them,—the special guidance of the Holy Spirit. So their message became not the word of man, but the word of God.

Miraculous power also belonged to the apostleship. For the establishment of Christianity it was necessary that miracles should be wrought. They were God's seals to its truth. Such wonderful works were therefore witnessed. The apostles spake in foreign tongues, healed the sick, raised the dead, and in other ways gave incontestable evidence that they wrought by the power of God. Speaking of his own ministry at Corinth, St. Paul writes, "Truly the signs of an apostle were wrought among you in all patience, by signs and wonders and mighty works."

It is evident that these qualifications for the

apostolic office did not exist after their day. Under Christ, they were the founders of the churches. To fulfill their important duties they were supernaturally endowed. With them passed away the peculiar prerogatives of the apostleship.

The *mission* of the apostles, the duties belonging to their office, were most important. They received their commission from the Saviour himself, with the assurance that they should do greater works than they had seen him do. Beginning at Jerusalem, they were to proclaim him to all nations as the true Messiah, the Saviour of a lost world. This was no easy task. On the one hand they were to encounter the inveterate prejudice and hostility of the Jews; on the other hand, the pride and paganism of the Gentiles. The Hebrew mind was in a state where it could not readily be reached. With the decline of that people's greatness, there was a decline of its piety. The majesty of the theocracy, whose imposing ceremonial and divine intervention had awed and restrained the popular mind, had long before passed away. The restraints of the monarchy were also withdrawn with its decline; while the passions and the will of that sensitive and imperious people were given unbridled indulgence. Civil feuds divided them and made them enemies the one to the other. Religious faction and fanaticism were carried to a strange excess, having nothing religious about them but the name. Besides all else, they chafed under the Roman yoke in a vassalage which they could not brook, but from which they could not free themselves. Fretted and excited and, more than all, maddened against Christianity by the fact that they had just stained their hands with the innocent blood of its Founder, the Jews were in a poor condition to hear the faithful teachings of the apostles.

Abroad, the prospect was hardly better. Enthroned in its ancient seats and sustained by the prejudices and selfishness of its priests, paganism held the nations in an iron tyranny. Its temples and altars stood firmly in every land. Its dark dominion embraced the world. Its pampered priesthood extorted the awe and service of the people. Kings and warriors were its vassals. Even in the most enlightened nations, where the Greek and Latin languages were spoken by sages and orators, where art was achieving its sublimest triumphs, all things were tributary to an overshadowing superstition. The employments of life, the customs of society, the education of the people, the sympathies of the popular mind, all circled around the debasing false worship as around a common center. Whether, therefore, we consider the mission of the apostles as among the Jews or among the Gentiles, we see that it was one requiring uncommon patience, prudence, fortitude, and faith. Above all, it required the co-operating energy of the Spirit of God.

The apostles undertook the great task. Inspired by the Holy Spirit, they were ready to undertake it. To the Jews they were prepared to announce their long-expected Messiah in the crucified and risen Jesus. To the pagans they were bold to declare the *unknown God* whom they worshiped in ignorance, and the way to him through the Lord Jesus Christ. Their great duty to all men was to preach the crucified and living Saviour. To do this effectively, they were empowered to work miracles whenever it was necessary to arrest the attention of men or to establish their own divine commission. Their duty led them to oppose the ceremonial and traditions of the Jews, the corrupting rites and worship of the pagans.

Another part of their mission was to gather into Christian communities all those who in every place could be influenced to renounce their wrong life and by faith to accept of Christ. Churches, simple in their organization, were therefore planted in the cities where the apostles were successful in their labors. These churches consisted of those who openly confessed Christ as their Lord and Saviour. Their members were united as brethren in fellowship for their own growth and in testimony before the unbelieving world. They chose their own teachers, adopted their own regulations, disciplined their own members, and exercised all the functions which belong to independent, sovereign commonwealths. The members of each church were the court of final appeal in cases of doubt and difficulty that arose amongst them. Their officers consisted of elders and deacons. The elders are also called bishops, overseers, pastors. They were the teachers of the churches, while the deacons were their assistants, attending more particularly to the secular affairs of the congregations. Speaking of this subject, the learned Mosheim remarks: "A bishop, during the first and second centuries, was a person who had the care of one Christian assembly, which, at that time, was generally small enough to be contained in a private house. He instructed the people, performed the several parts of divine worship, attended the sick, and inspected the circumstances and supplies of the poor."

The planting of such churches was a part of the apostolic work. Unlike the prophets, who sought to vitalize the ancient economy of the Hebrews, and through this to bring the people back to a spiritual life, the apostles rejected the old, and aimed to build up a new divine, permanent commonwealth, not confined to one people, but destined to embrace the world.

The *acts and success* of the apostles are a marked feature of this epoch. The death of Jesus was an era of moment in their lives. Before that event they had been learners; after it they became leaders. Before it they were weak, timid, ignorant; after it they were strong, bold, able to cope with the wisest. Especially did the Pentecostal baptism—when, as they were assembled in one place, a sudden sound as of a rushing tempest filled the house, and tremulous tongues, like sundered flames, rested upon the head of each one there—date the commencement of a new life for the apostles. That was the manifest descent of the Comforter whose presence Christ had promised. The apostles went forth from the sanctuary inspired men, with a new sense of their work and with new ability to discharge it. To the multitudes who had come up to the feast of Pentecost "from every nation under heaven," they proclaimed, in various languages, "the mighty works of God." Christ, crucified and risen, was the central theme of their discourse. Boldly did the apostles charge upon the Jews the guilt of being the murderers of Christ; clearly did they maintain that he whom they had slain was none other than their Lord and Christ.

The first apostolic sermon, preached in the most extraordinary circumstances, was a marked illustration of the power of the gospel and of the influence of that divine Agent who was thenceforth to attend it. The vast multitude was convicted of sin; the question, which since that time has been asked wherever the gospel has been preached, was heard, "What shall we do?" and three thousand souls were on that day added to the disciples. Fear fell on the multitude; wonders and signs attested the divine authority by which the apostles acted. That was the beginning of great things for Christianity. In the name of Christ, miracles were wrought not less wonderful than those which marked the Saviour's ministry. His name, his cross, possessed a power over men which far surpassed the power of any other religion. Wherever the Christian converts went, there went an influence which wrought a change of life, a renovation of the individual and of society. A new power was acknowledged among the institutions and dominions of men—a power blessed, all-controlling, and destined, in the lapse of ages, to convert the world to Christ.

For some time, amidst alternate successes and discouragements, with persecutions on the one hand and the triumphs of the gospel on the other hand, the apostles continued their labors at Jerusalem. In open rebuke and defiance of both Jewish and Roman power they persisted in preaching the word. Within the Hebrew temple, where the forms of the ancient worship, impressive in their decay, still lingered; beneath the bulwarks of the castle of Antonia, where the iron warriors of Rome awed the turbulent populace and maintained the dominion of the all-grasping empire: they planted and nourished an institution which should survive when temple and empire should have passed away, whose worship should become the worship of all peoples, and whose dominion should embrace all nations.

But the time soon came when it was important that the gospel should be borne abroad, when to the Jews who were scattered throughout the world, and to the Gentiles who were dwelling in darkness, Christ should be made known. The wider and more thorough diffusion of the gospel was effected through a strange agency, through the malice of the enemies of the new faith. Stephen, a faithful preacher and a powerful reasoner, became their victim, the first in a long succession of martyrs to the Christian truth. The taste of blood produced the thirst for more, and a bitter persecution scattered the disciples abroad, where God had a work for them to do. To Peter, the first of the apostles, was revealed in a vision the great fact that the Gentiles were to be fellow-heirs with the Jews in the inheritance of Christ, a fact which was soon illustrated under his preaching in the house of Cornelius, an officer of the Roman government, when the Holy Spirit descended upon the Gentiles and they spake with tongues and magnified God.

From that time the labors of the apostles were widely extended. Peter traveled into the East, beyond the bounds of Roman conquest, amongst nations alien to the Hebrews, where oriental manners and customs prevailed, and for a while he made his residence in Babylon. Tradition informs us of the acts and successes of these early missionaries throughout a great part of the known world, from Gaul to India, from the barbarian regions of the North to the torrid clime of Ethiopia.

In this wide field of the apostolic work there was one portion which demanded a laborer of somewhat different qualifications from those of the twelve apostles. For that service Providence had raised up one, who, the son of Jewish parents, was also a free-born citizen of Rome and was educated in the best learning of his time. Tarsus was "no mean city." Enriched by the products of the highest existing civilization, distinguished for its schools and philosophers, as well as for the general intelligence of its citizens, rich in classic and historic associations, the favorite of Roman emperors, it was the suitable home of the youth whose future mission, as a preacher of the gospel, would lead him among the polished cities of Greece and even to plant the Church of Christ within the walls of imperial Rome itself. There the early years of the great apostle to the Gentiles were spent, learning from his parents, who educated him according to the strict observances of the straitest sect of the Jews, and from the scholarly people with whom he daily mingled, until, himself a stern Pharisee, and acquainted with the works of Grecian poets and philosophers, he was removed to Jerusalem and placed under the tuition of the celebrated Gamaliel, a teacher of the law and theology of the Hebrews. It was with no feelings of approbation that this ambitious and fiery student beheld the growth of Christianity. A three-stranded cord of strength bound and held him to a fierce opposition. As a free-born Roman citizen he was allied to that great heathen imperialism which was holding the scepter of the world, whose unconquered soldiers were asserting their dominance over barbarian and cultured people alike. As a Grecian scholar he felt the pride of human learning and gloried in what the wisdom of the schools and the studies of philosophy could do for the enrichment of mankind. As a Jewish bigot, rigidly taught in the tenets of that separate people, he looked with cherished aversion, with defiant and bitter scorn upon a religion that seemed to threaten the polity of his fathers. There was no man then living who had more in his birth and training and the quality of his mind and the peculiarities of his position to make him an uncompromising foe of Christianity. He was its bitterest inquisitor and persecutor.

A day came, in the progress of the new faith, which was critical and crucial. Would it stand the test of bloody martyrdom? One of its preachers, a man full of grace and power, at whose hands great wonders and signs were wrought, stood forth in such pre-eminence that it was determined to crush him. He was brought before a prejudiced council, in whose presence his face was as it had been the face of an angel. Unable to answer his able historical plea, they hurried him out of the city and stoned him to death. A proud young man, Roman by birth, Grecian by studious taste, Jew by religion, stood there consenting to that first Christian tragedy. "And the witnesses laid down their garments at the feet of a young man named Saul." This is our introduction to Saul. From that time the passion of persecution possessed him like a demon. He laid waste the church; he entered into every Christian house; he dragged men and women to prison. He breathed threats and slaughter against the disciples of the Lord. He determined, by fierce and fiery strokes, to extirpate the new faith.

In the north of Syria stood the oldest city of the world. It had been renowned from the days of the patriarchs. It was called "The Eye of the East." It looked forth on the great routes of the merchant caravans. It was the rich center of trade and wide-reaching commerce. The merchant princes of the Orient came up to its prolific marts. Loaded caravans traversed its streets. The "rivers of Damascus" were famed for their purity and coolness. Flowing from Lebanon, they carried fertility and beauty to the city whose white dwellings shone in the eastern sunshine amidst gardens of roses of royal tints and flowers in wealthy variety. It was a sight worth going far to see in that day, as it is in this day.

Against that city of marvelous wealth and beauty, where the gospel was gaining a strong foothold, this ardent persecutor leveled his onset. With his fierce retainers, he spurred along the hard Roman roads for one hundred and thirty-six miles, until, on a sunny noon, as his cavalcade gained an eminence, that splended city burst on their view, an oasis of beauty, set like a gem in the gray and blazing desert.

Suddenly a light brighter than the fiery sun of the desert flashed upon him. Before it he and his company fell to the ground, and a question of arrest rang on his startled ear. Not for that had he left Jerusalem. Yet, perhaps, all the way the face of the transfigured martyr had been haunting him and the voices of the women and children whom he had cruelly wronged had echoed in his soul. The last words that he had heard from the martyr were words of trust in Jesus. The first words that he now heard from heaven in response to his anxious question, "Who art thou, Lord?" were, "I am Jesus whom thou persecutest." He was convicted, and his sins stood out before him. His Saviour, contrary to whom he had thought he ought to do many things, was revealed to him. A great revolution took place in all his thoughts and feelings, purposes and life. The voice that spoke to him from heaven was in "the Hebrew tongue," his own mother tongue, the language of the Christians whom he had hunted, the language of the expiring martyr as he had prayed with his last breath, "Lord, lay not this sin to their charge." It went home to Saul's inmost soul. It announced the fact which he would most like to forget. It told him of a living truth that he was trying to ride down and stamp out. It put first that which he would put last. He believed in heaven, though he did not believe in Christ. But out of heaven came the thrilling message, "I am Jesus!" It was irresistible. From the depth of his being came the overwhelming cry, sweeping, like a flood, all before it, "Lord, what wilt thou have me to do?" That settled the matter. It was an entire surrender. It carried Saul over from one side to the other. It changed the persecutor into an apostle.

The sight of the glory struck Saul blind, and for three days he was shut up within himself. He was in golden Damascus, but its outward beauties were hidden to him: another beauty was unfolding itself to his restored soul. Seeing nothing of this world, he came to sight of things of the other world. For all these days this question echoed in Saul's mind: "Why persecutest thou ME?" The *Me* became great, all-absorbing; it filled the whole horizon of his thought and covered the sunless heaven of his imagination. That

Me had been of small account, had been hated, had been a name of contempt and ignominy. It rose like a sun at morning, clear on his inner vision, waxing in volume of light and luster until it filled all the firmament with its burning glory. Thereafter there was but *one Name*—Jesus was all. The *Me* who was revealed on the high-road to Damascus was he whom Saul had persecuted. In the thought of what he had been doing he lived over his whole life. His early days, his education, the Scriptures of his nation, and their hopes and their forlorn fate, passed before him. The new faith, the wonder of Calvary, the story of the resurrection and the ascension, the miracles and the preaching of the apostles, the advice of Gamaliel at whose feet he had sat, the tragic martyrdom of Stephen, the prisons he had filled with the Lord's disciples, his ride across Palestine, and his fierce errand at Damascus, crowded his blind days of fasting. Then Christ was revealed. Saul saw that there was pardon and peace in him. It was not by human intervention he had been arrested. It was by the Lord himself.

Straightway there fell from his eyes as it were scales. He had the full vision of the Lord. From that darkened room he walked forth into unclouded day, the day of devoted service. The conversion was one that carried the whole man with it. He was a new man: old things had passed away; all things had become new. Paul's new birth was a birth into complete Christian life. He committed himself, soul and body to the Lord Jesus. Immediately he confessed his faith and was "with the disciples." He abandoned forever his old associates and his old habits and opinions, and boldly proclaimed Jesus. We are not surprised to read that he "increased the more in strength." Chrysostom says of him, "Christ, like a skillful physician, healed him when his fever was at the worst." It was a thorough healing.

The conversion of Paul was complete, and made him thenceforward to be Paul, the great apostle, the self-sacrificing, heroic soldier of the cross. Think of what he renounced! He was a man of liberal learning, which might have placed him amongst the foremost of his nation. All that learning he consecrated to Christ. He was, probably, a member of the Sanhedrin and therefore in the place of power. All that power he consecrated to Christ. He was where he might have gained wealth and fame. He allied himself to a sect that was everywhere spoken against and was despised, and he became its foremost advocate. He was a partaker of Christ's sufferings. He breathed *love*.

There is something very beautiful in his wish *to see Peter*. He had seen Christ: he wanted to see Christ's friend. He had been, for three years in the theological school of the desert, where he unlearned the old past of his education and had begun the study of the new faith. Coming again into the fellowship of the brethren and feeling the excitements of the great conflict between the old faith and the new, he desired to become acquainted with the leader of the Church, and he traveled back over the old route from Damascus to Jerusalem, and for fifteen days those two great apostles were together in the home of Peter. We can only imagine their conversations and their prayers with one another. Peter took Paul to his heart, and Paul was made strong and happy by his welcome. Ananias called him "Brother Saul." Barnabas took him by the hand and introduced him to the company of the apostles. Peter received him into his own home, as if he were an old friend. All the brethren cared for him, watched over him, thwarted his enemies, and rejoiced with him in all that he could do for Christ. From that time commenced a career full of marvel, full of human courage and divine benediction.

Behold the new defender of the truth, the powerful preacher of the gospel! In the synagogue of Damascus, to the amazement of all who heard him, he maintained the Messiahship of Christ. Against strong antagonists he battled for the Church which he once sought to destroy. The fiery soul of that learned Jew, with all its daring and power, was consecrated to Jesus of Nazareth.

A great work was to be done, and a great soul was needed for it. Paul set forth on his apostleship. In Jerusalem, the city that he loved, where he had passed pleasant years as a pupil of Gamaliel, where he had been known as the fiercest opponent of the despised Nazarene, he boldly spoke for his new Master. That, however, was not Paul's appointed place of labor. God had destined him for another sphere. He was to be the apostle to the Gentiles. After spending some years in his native city, Tarsus, he was called to labor at Antioch, where the gospel had already met with signal success. From that time he was in labors more abundant. His life became a succession of masterly and untiring efforts, followed by brilliant triumphs for the gospel. From the eastern coast of the Mediterranean, along the shores of the Ægean, to Italy, he proclaimed Christ as the Saviour of men. His first missionary tour led him to Cyprus and to the southeastern portion of Asia Minor; his second, to the northern and western portion till he reached the spot where Troy was. A call came across the blue Ægean from Macedonia, "Come over and help us," and Paul hastened to plant the standard of the cross on the soil of Europe. Oh, could the eye of the apostle have glanced through coming ages and could he have read a prophecy of the nations, and known how Europe, then enshrouded in the deep darkness of paganism, should one day become the seat of powerful Christian states, whose people also should fill another hemisphere with Christian institutions, how would his heart have still more exulted in the glorious mission which he had undertaken! Paul the first preacher of the gospel in Europe! Who so worthy as he to introduce the knowledge of Christ to the occidental nations! to become the predecessor of the loyal and learned propagators of Christianity in the countries that are the rulers of the world! While the oriental churches have fallen or have become mournfully corrupt and inefficient, has not the spirit of Paul lingered most in those of the West?

Among the most interesting scenes in the life of this greatest apostle are those which present us with his labors and successes in the great and splendid cities of that age, as at Athens, at Corinth, at Ephesus, and at Rome. Within these august and powerful capitals, where learning, art and opulence had their chosen seats, idolatry also had most securely and firmly entrenched and enthroned itself. It was allied to the state and to the schools, and it held to its support the business, the prejudices, and the pleasures of the people. It was no slight task, nor one free from hazard, to attack this guarded and cherished paganism.

It was therefore a noble and impressive scene, one which the artists have wrought with fine effect —*Paul addressing the men of Athens.* Before the high court of the Areopagus, amidst the sages and scholars of that academic city, surrounded by the gorgeous monuments of Athenian pride, power, and art—the splendid shrines, the columned temples, and, more imposing than all, the world-famed Parthenon, crowned with the lofty statue of Athens' guardian goddess, at the sight of which the joyous exiles wept as, after years of absence, they returned again to their native city— the apostle boldly and impressively declared the great truths which Plato dimly foresaw and which Socrates would have gladly welcomed, with an eloquence which vied with that of Athens' greatest orator.

Corinth was at that time in the zenith of her glory: enriched by the commerce of surrounding peoples, graced and beautified by her own magnificent works of art and by that elaborate architecture which for two thousand years has perpetuated the Corinthian name. At the same time she was at the nadir of her wickedness: filled with luxury, corrupt with vices, and given up to a debasing idolatry. There and at Ephesus, then the metropolis of Asia and the center of a most polluting worship, Paul proclaimed the gospel, and planted Christian churches into which he gathered many converts.

For a long time before he was permitted to enjoy the privilege, he longed to visit Rome also, that he might preach the gospel in that center of power and greatness. He desired that Christ should be known in that illustrious capital of the world, and he was willing to encounter all that was necessary to secure that object. He knew what extensive influence would be wielded by a city whose conquering arms were irresistible, whose dominion extended from the pillars of Hercules to the Euxine, from the forests of Gaul and the white cliffs of Britain to the shadows of Mount Atlas and the cataracts of the Nile, and within whose walls were gathered men illustrious in literature, jurisprudence, and art. Providence brought the veteran apostle to Rome, and his heart was gladdened by the success of the gospel there, even within the household of Cæsar. It was at Rome, in the calm evening of his toilsome and turbulent life, that he wrote those beautiful and pathetic words to his son Timothy, "I am already being offered, and the time of my departure is come. I have fought the good fight, I have finished the course, I have kept the faith: henceforth there is laid up for me the crown of righteousness, which the Lord, the righteous judge, shall give to me at that day: and not only to me, but also to all them that have loved his appearing." This may be considered as the dying testimony of that most remarkable man, that most laborious apostle.

Next to the name of Christ on the records of Christianity stands the name of Paul. There may have been greater men than Paul. We recognize the imperial place of Plato; the mysterious sway of Confucius; the genius of Homer. Conquerors, philosophers, philanthropists, there have been, from time to time, who have impressed the world, who have molded institutions and laws and human thought—great men in their day and way, but who have passed and whose work has not had the one quality of *imperishableness*. Paul laid foundations which have remained and are permanent. The churches, indeed, which he planted have not all survived; but as under the ruins and rubbish on which modern cities are builded the workmen come to the massive blocks on which old walls, old temples, old structures of various kinds, stood, so the eternal truths, on which the lapsed churches were founded, remain, and on the very places of their ancient rise and glory the revived, restored churches of Christ are again replanted; while all abroad, in new lands and among other peoples, those truths, through the undying words of Paul, have been through all the Christian ages building up permanent forces in the wide world.

The service of this great man was a ministry of the Lord Jesus. That was the inward charm of it. That was the light that shone in it like the clear light of gems. That gave the glory to his wonderful career. Christ was in Paul, and the life that he lived in the world was the life of Jesus. The gold that was woven into the royal fabric of his being was the love of Christ. He knew what he owed to the Saviour, and to him Christ was all in all. In the capitals of the world, where Cicero had addressed the Roman senate and where Demosthenes had delivered his matchless Oration for the Crown, Paul spoke on higher themes and for grander issues than theirs. On the track of the great empire the iron prows of whose galleys had plowed their victorious way from the surf of the Atlantic beyond the Hellespont, and the scream of whose eagles had been heard from the remotest Occident to the boundaries of the empire of Alexander in the Orient, he planted the germs of a wider sovereignty and saw the hopeful beginnings of a purer dominion. He left to the succeeding centuries the testimony of his peerless consecration, while his living LETTERS are a legacy which rank him as the chief of the glorious company of the apostles.

Little is known of the deaths of the apostles. Something is told us of their lives, and that is by far the more important. Some of them died at the hands of cruel men, but they counted not their lives dear unto themselves; they rejoiced to suffer and even to die for the name of Christ. They were ready to meet their Teacher and Friend, their beloved Saviour, and it mattered little to them when the summons should call them to his presence. In the vision which John had of the heavenly Jerusalem he saw that the walls of that glorious city had twelve foundations, and that in them were inscribed the names of the twelve apostles of the Lamb. It is through their fidelity and service that the heavenly city is one of security and strength for the disciples of Christ.

The years of their ministry were most marked for the victories of Christianity. Originating, under Christ, the vast project of the world's redemption, they entered upon the work as one to be accomplished. It was a work that God had put into their hands and he expected them to do their duty. They did not pause to consider the obstacles and opposition which they were certain to encounter; they did not hesitate because they were few and feeble and because superstition and paganism were strong and strongly entrenched within ancient barriers of customs and selfishness; they did not waver because the wealth and learning of the world were not with them. They knew that God was with them; they felt the inspiration of the Holy Spirit moving them; they were confident that through Christ strengthening them they could do all things. The results of their devotion and sacrifice were monumental. Within thirty years after the ascension of Christ, Christianity had become one of the most powerful of existing religions. It had superseded to a great extent the ancient Hebrew economy, had overthrown in its triumphant career long-established paganism, and had gained a firm foothold in the most important capitals of the earth, even in imperial Rome itself, the mistress of the world. It then became apparent that there were agencies connected with this new religion sufficient to supplant other institutions and dominions and to secure its universal and final triumph.

The apostolic epoch passed away; but the work which the apostles began went forward and is still advancing. We are summoned to emulate their example. Still is borne to our ears the cry which rolled over the Ægean, from the realm of Alexander to the silent chambers of the apostle Paul, "Come over and help us!"

EPOCH VIII.

OF THE HOLY SPIRIT.

OF THE HOLY SPIRIT.

THE agency of the Holy Spirit amongst men is probably confined within no limited epoch of their history. His work began with the commencement of man's moral being, and it will end only with the termination of the human race. Yet the more particular manifestation of the Spirit as a distinct and active Agent in the affairs of the world belongs to the period succeeding the ascension of Christ. Before that time men did not know that there was a Holy Ghost. He had energized in the ancient saints, he had spoken through the prophets, he had inspired the writers of the ancient Scriptures, he had striven with the sinners of the olden time and had been vexed by them, and by his agency a godly seed had been continued from age to age, through the earlier divine dispensations. Yet his ministration was not of that distinctive character by which it was marked on and after the day of Pentecost. There had been outward appliances, sacrifices, ceremonial observances, visible splendors, voices, visits of angels, visions, by which men were gained to God and kept near and loyal to him. The fact of the Trinity had not been made known: this belonged to a later revelation.

In opposition to the polytheism of the Gentiles, and to check the polytheistic tendencies of the Jews, Jehovah had been announced as the one only living and true God, and the fact of his *unity* had been kept clearly before, and impressed strongly upon, the fickle Hebrew mind. Although there had been some obscure intimations of a pluralism in this one Godhead, before the coming of Christ, yet it was not till the New Testament times that the revelation was made of the three persons in one God.

A new dispensation began: a fuller revelation to men of the Godhead took place; the bonds and ritual of the old theocracy passed away; the Holy Spirit became a recognized factor in the progress of the kingdom of God; he became a Shekinah within every man, and his still, small voice spake to every soul. No longer were the blessings of the covenant to be confined to a particular people, nor was God to be acceptably worshiped only on Mount Moriah or on Gerizim. There was to be a broader economy. The blessings which Christ had purchased by his all-embracing atonement were to be borne to all men by the all-prevalent Spirit. So direct and palpable and powerful were to be the manifestations and operations of the Holy Spirit under the new economy that it would be considered as the dispensation of the Third Person of the Godhead, and so intimately and efficiently was his agency to be connected with the means to be employed for the conversion of the world, that they were unitedly to be designated as the Ministration of the Spirit.

On the night of his betrayal, amidst the solemnities and sorrows of that sacramental occasion, when Jesus mysteriously announced to his beloved disciples the gloomy events that were before him, he took occasion to tell them of another Comforter, who, in his place, should abide with them after he should have gone away. He said, " It is expedient for you that I go away: for if I go not away, the Comforter will not come unto you; but if I go, I will send him unto you.... When the Comforter is come, whom I will send unto you from the Father, even the Spirit of truth ... he shall bear witness of me.... When he, the Spirit of truth, is come, he shall guide you into all the truth.... The Comforter, even the Holy Spirit, whom the Father will send in my name, he shall teach you all things, and bring to your remembrance all that I said unto you." To this divine Agent thenceforward was to be entrusted the superintendence and prosecution of the work of the world's redemption. He is the Spirit of power. He convinces the world of sin. He sanctifies those who believe in Christ. He searches the deep things of God. He produces effects like those of Pentecost.

It is plain from the Scriptures that the Holy Spirit is a *distinct, divine, personal Agent*. The doctrine of the Trinity sets forth the existence of one divine Being in three separate Persons, the same in substance, equal in power and glory: the Father, the Son, the Holy Spirit. As the Father and the Son have each his part in the work of human recovery, so also has the Spirit his part. His *personality* is proved by those statements which ascribe to him personal attributes and acts, not perhaps as expressing all that is true, but expressing all that we know to be true; his *divinity*, by those expressions which predicate of him divine attributes and works; his *distinct personality*, by those statements which assign to him certain offices of his own and separate from those of the Father and the Son. Thus, "The Comforter, even the Spirit of truth, whom I will send unto you from the Father." Again, there is the Father who sends him; the Son in whose place he is sent; the Holy Spirit who is sent. The analogy of language would seem to make the distinction lucid and conclusive.

The Saviour had a particular mission to fulfill; a work of instruction and of suffering to finish, during his brief and eventful ministry. When this was over his place in heaven summoned him back. What those things are which employ in heaven the Second Person of the Godhead we know only in part. But the Scriptures have given brief hints which are sufficient to assure us that his ascension was of more value to us than his personal presence here would have been. " When he ascended on high ... he gave gifts unto men." He left these fields of conflict and hardship, but it was as a conqueror returning in triumph to his capital and distributing the spoils of victory. In his Father's realm he is preparing places for his earthly friends. In the presence of God he ever liveth to make intercession for them. He is our Advocate at the throne.

His bodily presence on earth would have confined his agency to a limited portion of the Church. While his disciples were few in number and were together, he could do all that was necessary for them; but when the little band should become powerful and numerous communities, when the handful of corn in the earth on the top of the mountains should have fruit which would shake like Lebanon, when churches should be planted throughout the empire and in lands east and west where the Roman eagles never flew, then there would be need of a Presence in all those multiplied and separated churches—need of One who should everywhere strengthen and encourage the ministers of the word, give efficacy to the truth, open dark and depraved minds to conviction, and carry on to its completion the good work begun in the redeemed.

The personal presence of Jesus on earth would have been likely to prevent true views of the spirituality of his kingdom. The Hebrew mind was filled with aspirations for a temporal prince. Notwithstanding all his instruction to the contrary, the disciples of Christ, through his whole life, even after his resurrection and until his ascension, were looking for the restoration of their ancient kingdom to Israel. Had he remained on earth, gross and earthly views would have been developed amongst his followers. When their Leader had left them, they saw that they were alone, feeble men; that no secular arm was to be nerved in their behalf; that their reliance must be upon the divine, spiritual Helper whom the Saviour had promised to them. Then they began to feel that the Spirit of the Master was in ceaseless antagonism to the spirit of the world, and that he was to bring down a heavenly life to man. To come to the understanding of this truth was a great experience then; is a great thing now. There was needed, and always will be needed, the teaching of the Holy Spirit. There is a powerful influence in the invisible existence of Christ, in the invisible agency of the Holy Spirit. The presence of Jesus as a true man might have produced familiarity. Men would have thronged around him, as they did during his earthly ministry; they would have deserted their homes, their business, their country, for the sake of being with the Master, of listening to his gracious words, of witnessing his stupendous works, of sharing his divine gifts. Now he is exalted to the throne of heaven. We supplicate, we praise, we adore, we serve.

So much, at least, may be said as showing why it was better that Jesus by his departure, should make way for the advent and presence of the Holy Spirit, than that he should personally remain on earth. But the whole subject is not brought before us till we consider the peculiar *office-work of the Holy Spirit*. He came to take the place of Christ, to do for the disciples what the Saviour would have done could he have been personally present with them. To every believer, in every place, throughout all time, he was to give that aid, encouragement, solace, which the blessed Saviour would have given by his words, looks, personal sympathy, divine power. Over all Christian communities, in all lands, in the strong, mature churches of enlightened states, in the feeble, struggling churches in the midst of surrounding superstition and paganism, he was to maintain a vigorous, guardian superintendence, increasing their members from without, increasing their graces from within. To him was entrusted the kingdom of God on earth, in all its multiplied organizations and powerful agencies. He was to sanctify the ministry and its membership; to give efficacy to its written and preached word; to go with its heralds from land to land— in a word, to make the gospel, in its varied influences and ministries, the wisdom of God and the power of God to the salvation of the world.

His office-work was to be not only in and through the churches of Christ, but also directly upon the souls of men; convincing them of their own sinfulness, of their relation to a righteous God, and of a coming retribution, and leading them to repentance and faith in the Lord Jesus Christ. Wherever there was a soul fallen, estranged by sin from God, there was to be the field of the Spirit's work. The world in its woes, to the extent of its wretchedness, is the only limit to his divine operations. The salvation of the world is the object of the Spirit's work, as it was the object of the Redeemer's work. As Christ tasted death for every man, so the agency of the Spirit is for every man.

His office-work is therefore partly a work of *renewal*. The mind that was depraved, perverted, lost to God and averse to goodness, is brought to love God, to delight in his service, to be holy. This renewal of individual minds, by the influence of the Holy Spirit, is the great process by which the world is to be converted to God.

It is also partly a work of *sanctification*. Those who are renewed he leads on to higher attainment in holiness, to a closer union with God. He becomes their Instructor. He takes of the things of Christ and shows them to his people, unfolding to them the excellence of God, the beauty of holiness, the loveliness of the Christ-like spirit. He becomes also their Helper, guarding them from dangers and the assaults of foes, and delivering them out of all their temptations, trials, conflicts. "He helpeth our infirmities."

He cultivates in us the spirit of prayer, of child-like faith, so that we can look up confidently to God in all our distresses, and look forward cheerfully to the rest that remaineth for his people. Thus is the promise of Jesus fulfilled, "I will not leave you orphans."

The history of the Church testifies to the *value and preciousness* of the Spirit's presence. Whereever the gospel has gone in its wide influence and triumphs, there the Holy Spirit has gone with it to make the truth mighty to the pulling down of strongholds. Nay, he has gone before the gospel, preparing the heart to receive it, as the soil is prepared for the scattered seed. He has worked in the hearts of the children of disobedience, causing them to reflect and awakening them to consider their souls' salvation. He has carried forward the work of sanctification, in the souls of believers, until death has been swallowed up in victory. Confined by no material trammels, the omnipresent and omniscient Spirit has awakened every troubled convicted sinner, has been the Comforter of every child of Christ. His agency has been manifest in the awe that has pervaded wide communities, in the confessions of penitence at unnumbered altars, in the vows of obedience before the Searcher of all hearts, in the lives of sacrifice and holiness read and known of all men.

Wider and richer *results* are yet to come. Under his divine guidance the word is to go forth with power in all lands, and the world is to be converted. The ministration of the Spirit will be still more glorious. Mind shall be disenthralled.

The bondage of corruption shall cease. All men shall be brought into the glorious liberty of the children of God.

A glance at some of the more marked results of the Spirit's agency will be sufficient to demonstrate the glory of his ministration, to prove that it is much more glorious than any that has preceded it.

According to the instructions of the Master, his apostles returned from Olivet to Jerusalem to await in meditation and prayer the promised advent of the Spirit. In a marked manner the promise was fulfilled. On the day of Pentecost, when they were all with one accord in one place, there came a sudden sound from heaven, like the rush of a tempest, which filled the house where they were assembled. At the same time, emblematic of the divine presence, tongues of fire flamed from the head of each of them, tokens of that wonderful power in the use of human languages which they were to receive as the direct gift of God. At once they felt the energy of that divine Agent who had been promised, and they were miraculously endowed with the gift of tongues. To the temporary dwellers in Jerusalem, who had come up from "every nation under heaven" to the sacred feast, they began to publish the gospel of Christ. Then followed the first, and in some respects the most remarkable, revival of the new dispensation, characterized by phenomena similar to those which have since been witnessed in what are called, in memorial of this event, pentecostal seasons. The truth presented by the apostles was carried home by the Spirit to the minds which he had awakened to receive it. Some who but a few days before, possibly, were shouting with the Jewish rabble, "Crucify him!" were now convicted of their sins, and tremblingly asked, "Brethren, what shall we do?" Out of the vast multitude who on that day listened to the preaching of the cross, three thousand souls accepted Christ. Such was the glorious commencement of the Spirit's ministration. In all their future labors the apostles were blessed with the presence of the Holy Spirit, who gave the gospel its marvelous efficacy, so that Jewish prejudice and intolerance and Gentile pride and paganism gave way before it, while the humbling religion of Jesus became aggressive and dominant. For a while it seemed as though the power of the Spirit would carry all before it.

Centuries of darkness had rolled over the world before the morning light of the Reformation dawned. Learning was locked in the cells of hooded monks, while ignorance blindly led the multitude. Faction and fanaticism widely prevailed. The fiat of the Pontiff, the terrors of the Inquisition, awed the nations. It seemed as though earth's darkest night would know no morning, as though the tyranny of Rome could not be broken. But the Holy Spirit began his work. Quietly, in the cloister of a thoughtful monk, he awakened profound interest in the great truths of revelation. On the dusty shelves of the University of Erfurth lay a Latin Bible. To that book the Spirit guided the hand of the thoughtful student and clearly illuminated the word of God to his mind, so that he longed for the way to Christ and to salvation.

The great work of the Reformation was the work of the Holy Spirit. He led Luther out of the bondage of the papacy and commissioned him as the eminent apostle of the reform. That work of the sixteenth century will ever stand as a demonstration of the wonderful agency of the Spirit in the minds of men. The world awoke as from the nightmare of ages. The power of the papacy was broken, and what it lost has never been regained. Nations threw off their vassalage to the papal see, and the Pontiff who had put on crowns or displaced them at his will became the harmless bishop of Rome. With the wide revival of religion came also the renaissance of learning and art. Through every department of life in many lands the Reformation sent the shock of its influence, an influence which shall not cease till Christ's churches everywhere shall stand forth in that freedom wherewith Christ makes his people free.

It was the work of the Spirit which gave Puritanism its start and steady growth in the seventeenth century, and which led on to the development of those principles of religious and civil liberty which have made Great Britain and the United States the seats of spiritual and benevolent churches and which have made those nations foremost in all that is truly great and worthy.

It was the work of the Spirit which led to "the great awakening" of the eighteenth century whose power extended through northern Europe and the English colonies of America, when Whitefield and Wesley in England, and Edwards and the Tennents in America, were the apostles of the triumphant gospel of Christ. Then a new era in the history of the churches commenced. On a broad extent of territory an unwonted solemnity and a spirit of inquiry prevailed. Religion became the all-engrossing subject of thought and conversation on the part of multitudes, so that in many instances secular duties were neglected, and it became necessary for pastors to remind members of their flocks of that part of the command, "Six days shalt thou labor, and do all thy work." Christians were revived and sinners were awakened. Itinerant preachers, like Whitefield and Tennent, went from place to place, declaring with a pungency and power like that of the ancient prophets, the messages of God. "The doctrines of grace" were pointedly presented to the congregations, and the word of God became "living, and active ... and piercing even to the dividing of soul and spirit ... and quick to discern the thoughts and intents of the heart." On some occasions, hundreds under a single discourse were hopefully converted and within a few years tens of thousands were united to the visible Church of Christ, and the pentecostal days seemed to have returned again.

The precious revivals of the nineteenth century, those works of grace in which we have shared, are also the work of the Holy Spirit. They have been witnessed by all the world: not merely in Christian communities, but in the old realms of paganism—wherever, upon continents or islands of the sea, missionaries have planted the cross.

The new development of personal devotion to Christ among the young, which has banded millions of youthful disciples in covenant and earnest endeavor for Christ and the Church has been evidently marked by the leadings of the divine Spirit.

It is the work of the Spirit to extend the triumphs of the gospel, to bring on the fulfillment of ancient prophecy respecting the universal reign of Christ on earth. That is indeed a glorious ministration which is to secure the emancipation of the world from sin, which is to usher in the dayspring from on high, and to bring forward the noontide glories of the promised and long-awaited Millennium.

EPOCH IX.

THE MILLENNIAL.

THE MILLENNIAL.

For nineteen hundred years the Church of Christ has looked forward to the Millennium. That golden age of prophecy, brighter in the distant future than the golden age of the past of which the poets have sung, sweeter with its paradise regained than was the paradise which was lost, early caught the gaze of the Christian seer, before whom, among the rocky peaks of Patmos, was unrolled the long history of the Church through her conflicts and trials and triumphs. In the dark days of the early militant Church, when the sword of persecution was unsheathed against it and the strong arm of power wrought to cast it down, it was the thought of that coming time of peace and glory which sustained the disciples in their toils and sufferings. Cheeringly to the vision of the martyr rose the sublime prospect of a prosperous epoch when the earth shall become the undisputed inheritance of the saints and there shall be none to vex them. Soothingly, like the harmonies of celestial minstrelsy, fell upon the ear of the dying believer the sweet strains as of multitudinous voices jubilant through that coming period whose dawn he had hoped to see. As the ages have gone on faith in the good time that is coming has not wavered, but still the watchers from afar have seen its light streaming up the sky, as dwellers on hills and mountain-sides have seen the gleams of the morning on the remote horizon. In the hastening on of that time pious men of every generation have joyfully labored, in full confidence that He who has promised will in his own wisdom bring it to pass. The hope of the Millennium is alive and active now in the minds of the people of God as truly as at any former period; so that some are even cherishing the fond expectation that they shall live within the time of the Millennial reign of Christ.

The belief of the Church respecting this epoch of its history has not been uniform. Quite commonly it has not been considered as a result of the ordinary and natural development of the kingdom of God through processes of instruction and growth such as are usually employed, but rather as a special bestowment of victory and glory by a direct divine interposition. It was very natural that the Jews who were converted to Christianity should retain many of the Hebrew notions respecting the Messiah. Accordingly, we find very early traces of the belief in the personal reign of Christ at a coming period—a literal interpretation of those passages of the sacred Scriptures which in glowing poetry and high-wrought figures describe that event. As early as the second century, this theory became a prevalent doctrine, and high names among the fathers of that age are enrolled in its defense. Although this view has been more or less modified by the character and education of the minds that have embraced it, it is still widely maintained, and is now one of the two great theories on this subject between which the faith of Christians is divided.

It sets forth the fact that the Lord shall visibly appear and reign upon the earth, with all his saints, for a thousand years, in splendor and enjoyment beyond anything which has before been known. It is claimed by some that at his second advent the righteous dead shall be raised, and that after the thousand years, there shall be the resurrection of the wicked and the final judgment of the world. Gross and sensuous views have sometimes been entertained of the millennial state which are utterly without warrant of the word of God. Fanciful ideas often have been propounded by writers in their discussion of the subject, to such a degree that minds of more sober and reflective cast have been repelled from any consideration of it.

A more just and scriptural opinion seems to be this: that the kingdom of Christ, through the agencies which have been and are being employed, shall at length become universally prevalent, and that then for a long period he shall exercise a spiritual dominion over the race; not that all souls will be converted, but so that, in a general way, it may be said that the world is converted.

This opinion, for two reasons at least, appears to be more correct than that which teaches the visible reign of Christ for a thousand years. First, it affords a rational interpretation to those passages of Scripture which are most confidently relied on for the latter opinion. It is not necessary to suppose that the apostle, where he speaks in the Apocalypse of the reign of Christ, intends a visible personal reign. His spiritual dominion, through the spread of the gospel, the glorious ministration of the Spirit, and the universal triumph of Christianity, fairly exhausts the meaning of his statements and is more in harmony with other teachings of the Scriptures. Secondly, this opinion does not conflict with those passages of Scripture which teach that the second advent of Christ will be for the judgment of the world. Christ represents that the design of his coming again in glory is not for the sake of reigning bodily on earth but for the sake of judging all nations. He says he will come again not to live with his friends in this world, but to take them to live with him in the places which he has prepared for them in the mansions of his Father. He tells of only one resurrection-time—that of the evil and the good.

Before Christ's ascension the apostles believed in a personal reign, but after they were enlightened by the Holy Spirit they seem to have looked and labored only for the spiritual sovereignty of their Master. They afterward taught that his coming would be for judgment; his descent would be with the voice of the archangel and with the trump of God; his eye would penetrate every soul and bring to light the hidden things of darkness; then, after judgment has been pronounced, cometh the end—the heavens to pass away with tumult, the earth with all its works to be burned, the righteous to ascend to be forever with the Lord.

Pleasant, therefore, as may be the illusion of the bodily reign of Christ, and gratifying as it may be to many minds to indulge in visionary conceptions concerning such an event, we do not seem to be warranted by the Scriptures in consenting to that view.

The *date* of the Millennium is unknown. Those who have wrought most assiduously at the Apocalyptic chronology cannot agree upon the time. It is not designed that they should. As early as the lifetime of St. Paul there were those who held that the second advent of Christ was near; and this opinion created alarm with some and caused others to renounce their worldly associations. The apostle wrote a letter to correct this error, and to teach, as other portions of the Bible also teach, that "of that day knoweth no man." The same thing is true of the beginning and the end of the Millennium. We do not know when its brilliant morning shall dawn upon the world, nor how long that splendid epoch shall continue.

It is a common opinion that the seventh millennary in the history of the world will constitute the biblical Millennium. As God originally appointed six days for labor, to be followed by the Sabbath, so it has been thought that six thousand years of sin may be followed by a thousand years of holiness, the Sabbath of the world's history. There is something natural and alluring in this theory, although there is nothing but this remote analogy to sustain it. Some have argued that the thousand years of Christ's reign should be reckoned as are other prophetical dates, a day for a year, which would make the millennial period to consist of three hundred and sixty-five thousand years. This view, full of comfort and inspiration, opens a grand prospect for the Church and for the world. It makes these preparatory periods of a few thousand years seem insignificant in contrast with that long period of more than paradisean glory and blessedness. Thus would the wisdom and benevolence of God in the government of the world stand out in striking characters, while the multitudes of the redeemed through those prolonged ages of peace and universal holiness would immensely surpass the numbers of the unsaved and greatly augment the apparent excellence and glory of the Saviour's work. Whether this shall be so or not must be left to the slow fulfillment of those predictions which abound in the word of God, but which appear to be left designedly obscure, so that they can be clearly interpreted only by the event.

The *coming on* of the Millennium will undoubtedly be slow and progressive and in the ordinary course of providence. We have no warrant for thinking that it will be miraculously ushered in, that violent and revolutionary overturnings will prepare the way for it, that the kingdom of God will be forced upon the nations. Its evolution will be normal and without observation. All things which are now taking place, the moral and political changes which are occurring, the benevolent and missionary movements of the Church, the pantings and struggles of the unevangelized peoples for improvement, are all preparatory to the final and complete triumph of the Christ. Slowly and surely the ancient and venerable dominions of paganism will be undermined, until at the appointed time they shall fall beyond recovery. Slowly and surely the principles of the gospel shall be planted like good seed in the soil of the nations, until, when in the good providence of God the springtime shall come, they shall germinate and ripen quickly for the glorious harvest.

We can form but a faint idea of the possible rapid spread and victories of the gospel, when the hindrances shall be removed and the mighty energies of the Spirit shall give efficacy to the labors of the churches. A nation shall then be born in a day. On the right hand and on the left, from the north and from the south, shall be heard the tidings of whole communities embracing the gospel of Christ. Days like that of Pentecost may be witnessed simultaneously in many quarters. What we have seen in small districts, during powerful revivals, that which we have seen in the success of the gospel among the Hawaiian people, among the Karens, may be but feeble illustrations of what is yet to take place on a comprehensive scale. Revivals may extend over continents, truth be joyfully embraced, error lose its power over the human mind, wide victories of grace wait on the agency of the Spirit, thousands and millions throng penitently and gladly to Christ as a welcome Saviour, and the world come over on to the Lord's side. All this may take place quietly, enmity and opposition being withdrawn and all souls coming to know the need and the worth of salvation, under the awe of God's recognized presence. If this be so, who can tell how soon the Millennium will dawn upon the world? While some now living shall be witnesses, the grand epoch may be ushered in. The seventh-thousand period may be that of the world's jubilee.

The *order of events* may be substantially gathered from the Scriptures: Christ shall gradually gain supremacy over sin, heathenism, and error; there shall be for a long period the universal diffusion of Christianity; after that for a season Satan shall prevail; then shall come the judgment, the end of the world, with the future allotments of the righteous and the wicked.

The *characteristics* of the Millennium must be derived solely from revelation. There is nothing in the nature of things, nothing in the logic of the situation, to prove that the gospel shall finally triumph. It has well been said, "The Millennium is a hieroglyph not yet solved." The analogy from past history would show that the victories of the truth are to be followed by mournful reverses, that whatever success it may gain, however hopeful may be its prospects, disaster is to tread hard after, and disappointing days are to follow. So was it after the successes of the apostolic times. So was it after Constantine had made Christianity the religion of imperial Rome. So was it after the Reformation and the great revivals of religion. So, but for the promises of God, the pledge of his aid, might it be in the future. Even now there are terrible indications that the magnificent work which has been heroically accomplished by our scholarly and judicious brethren in the planting of institutions of learning and religion at vast expense and sacrifice throughout the empire of the Sultan will be exterminated through the chicanery and fury of the unspeakable Turk. Human nature is prone to wrong-doing. Idolatry and superstition gratify the mind that does not like to retain God in its knowledge. As far as men are concerned, there is no assurance of the supremacy of Christianity; there is no bulwark in the nature or habits of the race strong enough to withstand the onsets of evil. The fact, therefore, of the Millennium, and its characteristics, must be learned from the word of God.

In the Bible an epoch is spoken of such as has not yet been witnessed. Indeed, from the earliest times, all along in the history of God's dealings with men, there is a succession of predictions of the most interesting character, expressed in a variety of forms, all pointing forward to a time that has not yet been known on earth. Hardly had the fall occurred, when the pledge was given and the prediction made that the seed of the woman should bruise the head of the serpent. This pledge is yet to be redeemed. Satan's power is to be broken; his dominion over men is to be destroyed; Christ is to reign supreme on earth; and then the prediction will be fulfilled. Parallel with this is another prediction, given more than four thousand years after the former, which says, that the old serpent, which is the Devil and Satan, shall be bound for a thousand years, and cast into the abyss, which shall be shut and sealed over him, that he should deceive the nations no more till the end of the thousand years. This event is still future: the thousand years are to come. Between these two strikingly similar predictions, so far asunder, are many others which describe the state of things on their fulfillment. It is written that God will give to his Son the nations for his inheritance and the uttermost parts of the earth for his possession; that all kings shall bow down before him, all nations shall serve him; that from the rising of the sun even unto the going down of the same God's name shall be great among the Gentiles; and in every place incense shall be offered unto his name and a pure offering; that the earth shall be filled with the knowledge of the glory of the Lord, as the waters cover the sea; that God has sworn by himself, that unto him every knee shall bow, every tongue shall swear; that the days are coming when they shall not teach every man his fellow-citizen, and every man his brother, saying, "Know the Lord," for all shall know him from the least to the greatest of them. It was prophesied by Daniel, "The kingdom and the dominion, and the greatness of the kingdoms under the whole heaven, shall be given to the people of the saints of the Most High: his kingdom is an everlasting kingdom, and all dominions shall serve and obey him." St. John, on the lonely watch-tower that loomed above the dark waters of the Ægean, heard great voices in heaven, saying, "The kingdom of the world is become the kingdom of our Lord, and of his Christ: and he shall reign forever and ever." These and numerous other statements of Scripture foretell a period such as has not yet been witnessed, and plainly indicate the coming Millennium.

Preëminently that epoch shall be one of *holiness*. Sin shall be banished from the world. If the passages which predicate universal holiness of that period are not to be taken as strictly literal in that respect, they may be fairly understood as teaching that the exceptions shall be so few as not to be regarded in a general statement. It is the reign of Christ over his saints. "In that day," it is predicted, "shall there be upon the bells of the horses, *Holy unto the Lord*." Religion shall be all-controlling; it shall influence men in every calling and relation of life. Idolatry, superstition, all forms of false worship, shall be done away. The mighty systems of imposture and paganism which, for ages, have held under their iron tyranny the vast majority of the human family, shall then be unknown. The misery and degradation consequent upon them, the pain and toils and dangers of penances and pilgrimages, shall be no more. In place of them shall be the pure worship of God, in the home, in the sanctuary, over all the world. The reign of sin on the earth has been long and fearsome. It has cursed the world and the dwellers upon it. Nature has felt the pain. It has planted the soil with thorns and briers. It has doomed man to the servitude of warring forces. Crime, lust, violence, madness, have sprung from it, and men have gone in long processions to a wretched future. The whole creation has groaned and travailed in pain together until now.

The gloomy bondage is to be broken: the fearful curse is to end; the earth is to become as the garden of God. Holy songs, like those of its early paradise, are to float up from its entire territory.

That epoch shall be one of *peace*. There shall be no more the armor of the armed man in the tumult, and the garments rolled in blood; plains piled with hecatombs of slaughtered men; ruins of pillaged and burned cities. Nations shall beat their swords into plowshares, and their spears into pruning-hooks; nation shall not lift up sword against nation, neither shall they learn war any more. Peace, and the general fruits of peace, shall prevail in every land. The time and capital and labor employed in the sustaining of armies and navies and fortifications and the manufacture of ammunition and arms shall be diverted into the channels of useful labor and to the promotion of human happiness. The ocean shall become the highway of a benevolent commerce. Trades, manufactures, agriculture, art, all science and business, shall have direct reference to the welfare of men. The skill of the artist, the learning of the scholar, the labor of the mechanic, the legislation of the statesman, every profession and employment, shall be consecrated to the true interests of the race and the glory of God. Homes, in their rural beauty; cities, in their vast magnificence; nations, in their intellectual and moral power; earth, in the greatness of its mighty population and the grandeur of its augmenting glories, shall exist in peace and harmony and without fear of violence.

That epoch shall be one of *knowledge*. Religion is the queen of learning. When her sway shall be complete, ignorance, the daughter of sin, shall be banished from the earth. When, at the time of the Reformation, religion was revived, learning also had revival. During the Dark Ages, when superstition ruled the nations, men were in ignorance fearful and profound, but no sooner had the trumpet-blast sounded from the cell of Erfurth than the mind of the nations was aroused, and science, art, and popular education were revived. It is in Christian states that true science and learning have their honored seats and secure their brightest successes. What, then, may we not expect when the reign of righteousness shall become universal, and when the minds of men shall be untrammeled by sin? Who shall say that the discoveries of modern science, the inventions and improvements of our age, already wonderful, are anything more than the faint foreshadowings of those works of genius, inventions in science, and employment of the slumbering forces around us, which shall be witnessed amidst the intelligent and splendid triumphs of the Millennium? What will hinder but that the acute mind shall discover new applications of the laws already known, more powerful forces within the arcana of nature, sublimer truths hitherto wisely concealed, so that works of strength and beauty and utility shall far surpass those which have heretofore been known?

There shall be the prevalence also of higher spiritual knowledge. The earth shall be full of the *knowledge of the Lord.* "In that day shall the deaf hear the words of the book, and the eyes of the blind shall see out of obscurity and out of darkness. . . . They also that err in spirit shall come to understanding, and they that murmur shall learn doctrine." Wisdom and knowledge shall be the stability of those times. The great truths of revelation shall come into clearer interpretation, while the deep things of God shall be made known by the Spirit to man.

That epoch shall be one of *prosperity* and *enjoyment*. Whereas adversity and pain have been the sad heritage of man, blessedness and material well-being shall then be his portion. The quietness and loveliness that indicate a state of happy prosperity are imaged to us in the scriptural description of the Millennial state: "The wolf shall dwell with the lamb, and the leopard shall lie down with the kid; the calf and the young lion and the fatling together; and a little child shall lead them." It is written that tears shall be wiped away from all faces, that the ransomed shall come to Zion with songs and everlasting joy upon their heads. Prophecy in glowing imagery describes the prosperous condition of that coming time, when the commerce and wealth of the sea shall be consecrated to God, when the opulence and power of the Gentile nations shall become tributary to the truth, while upon Israel a cloudless sun shall shine with perpetual radiance. Beyond all doubt the Scriptures teach that in company with the Gentile world, the ancient people of God shall enjoy the blessings of the Millennium. Though they may not be restored to their own land, the historic soil of Palestine, as for ages has been their hope, they shall be restored to the privileges and blessings of their forfeited covenant with God.

The *indications of the approach* of the Millennium are numerous. These indications are seen in *the decay of old systems of error*. The time was when those systems which have most widely prevailed were vigorous and aggressive. They sent forth their apostles; they entered upon careers of conquest; they converted nations to their faith. Brahmanism once had the vitality and energy necessary for its wide increase and prevalence. Buddhism was once marked by eminent growth and extension. Its missionaries went from land to land, over the mountain ranges of the Himalaya, and beyond the waters of the Indus, in the zeal of a vigorous propagandism. Mohammedanism, relying on carnal weapons, the fire and the sword, once forced itself upon the nations of Western Asia and became the religion of many wild and powerful tribes. But the days of conquest and extension of these various systems are past. Although still powerful, they are waning; the latest attempts at their revival are the spasms of dissolution; they are in their dotage; their deluded subjects are losing faith in them and reverence for them. Slowly and surely they are giving way before the power of truth and the agency of Providence. The lower forms of heathenism seem to be only awaiting a vigorous assault before they shall fall and pass away. In our own time there has been the extraordinary spectacle of a people anticipating the presence of missionaries by casting their idols to the moles and the bats. A divine influence is abroad in the earth, weakening the powers of darkness and bringing on a dissolution of their accursed sway.

If we turn to the corrupt forms of Christianity, we witness symptoms of decay or of a return to a purer faith. Roman Catholicism, though claiming immutability and infallibility, is becoming greatly modified in its theories and practices, has renounced, to a great extent, its crimes of persecution, has abolished the Inquisition, is favoring the use of the Bible by the laity, and is disposed to some measure of outward fellowship with those who are not of its communion. It has lost its ascendency in the more enlightened states, and even in Rome holds itself as a prisoner of the Italian government. The ancient oriental churches which long ago departed from the faith once for all delivered to the saints, have witnessed revivals of pure religion. In the Greek, Armenian, Nestorian, Syrian, and Coptic churches has been awakened a spirit of genuine religious inquiry, and in some cases their ecclesiastics have become the subjects of saving grace. We may anticipate with hope the regeneration of these ancient churches and the renewal of their old-time zeal in the spread of the gospel.

Indications of the approach of the Millennium may also be seen in the *wide success of Christian missions* and in *the determination of the followers of Christ to push to completion the conquests of the truth.* Many are abroad with the good news, and knowledge is increasing; the women that publish the tidings are a great host. The gospel is gaining firm foothold in many lands: the barriers of sin and superstition are falling before it; the word of God is read in every language; the means of grace are brought to bear upon all ages and classes of men. Christianity is ever aggressive. The crumbling of other systems indicates its more vigorous exertions. Close on the track of its retreating foes, it presses hard after, to gain what they have lost. Over the wreck and ruin of Satan's empire, it urges its way to the conquest of the world. Nothing less has ever been its aim; nothing less will satisfy its adherents. Every error must be supplanted by the life-giving truth. For this have its apostles toiled: for this have its martyrs died: for this has the contest been hotly and unceasingly waged, as the ages have rolled away. Its heralds are more widely scattered than ever before; its conquering hosts are abroad on every battle plain. They are piercing the old realms of night and summoning to yield the strong fortresses of sin. *The world!* THE WORLD! is their battle-cry, and it rings from land to land, as through watching and toiling victory follows victory.

The *fulfillment of prophecy* further indicates the approach of the Millennium. Through the dimness of ages the ancient seers beheld the radiance of a glorious day. The prophets declared the coming of a time when holiness and happiness shall prevail upon the earth. As the scroll of time has been unrolled, fulfillment has followed fulfillment, until we are drawing near the end. Empire after empire has risen and flourished and passed away, as the prophets predicted. One event has succeeded another according to their express declarations.

There are portents which indicate that dire events are near at hand. There are omens of good which assure us that God will overrule all things for the advancement of his holy Church. The changes of our day, the onward movements of the nations, the overthrow of old powers of darkness, the victories of the gospel, all are preparing the way of the Lord and hastening the arrival of the world's final jubilee. The day is to come when

"All the ends of the earth shall remember and turn unto the Lord: and all the kindreds of the nations shall worship before him."

Satan shall be bound; the reign of sin shall be ended; righteousness shall universally prevail. Mankind shall be united in one peaceful and happy family, dwelling in bonds of sympathy and brotherhood, and loving each his neighbor as himself. Earth shall be as a holy temple, resounding with songs of praise and gratitude.

To that splendid epoch of the world's Millennium all other epochs have been subsidiary. The march of God's purposes, in all their grandeur and sublimity, through the complex events of the slowly-passing ages, has been directly forward to that crowning result. For that, dispensation followed dispensation, governments rose and fell, and the whole history of the world transpired.

To that glorious epoch, we, with the saints of all ages, look confidently and longingly forward.

O Christ! hasten on thy Millennial reign—the reign of peace and holiness, and blessedness!

www.ingramcontent.com/pod-product-compliance
Lightning Source LLC
Chambersburg PA
CBHW021845230426
43669CB00008B/1087